All in One WOMAN

REVEALING THE GREATNESS WITHIN

Written By

Roberta Goffney

COPYRIGHT © 2020 BY ROBERTA GOFFNEY

ALL RIGHTS RESERVED. THIS BOOK OR ANY PORTION THEREOF MAY NOT BE REPRODUCED OR USED IN ANY MANNER WHATSOEVER WITHOUT THE EXPRESS WRITTEN PERMISSION OF THE PUBLISHER EXCEPT FOR THE USE OF BRIEF QUOTATIONS IN A BOOK REVIEW.

PRINTED IN THE UNITED STATES OF AMERICA

FIRST PRINTING, 2020

All in One WOMAN

REVEALING THE GREATNESS WITHIN

Written By

Roberta Goffney

DEDICATION

I dedicate this book to my family, friends, and every grandchild now and in the future who I may or may not get a chance to see. I pray this book gives you a few great tips as well as guidance. It is here to help you dodge many mistakes along your journey of life. Glams took the punch, so you do not have to.

For every woman and young lady, I pray this book enhances what you are doing or assists from this moment forward.

Mrs. Roberta Goffney, Author

CONTENTS

CHAPTER 1: The Girl Before the Woman 3
CHAPTER 2: Runaway 19
CHAPTER 3: The Drug Bust 35
CHAPTER 4: The Woman 39
CHAPTER 5: Mr. Mandingo 47
CHAPTER 6: Family 60
CHAPTER 7: Trouble in My Way 81
CHAPTER 8: Babysitter 94
CHAPTER 9: Misunderstanding and Illness 112
CHAPTER 10: Teacher in the Ministry 123
CHAPTER 11: The Power of Change 135
CHAPTER 12: Amazing Husband Part 1 & 2 142
CHAPTER 13: Dazzling Daughters 148
CHAPTER 14: A Little "Peace" of Me 166
CHAPTER 15: Revealing the Greatness Within 182

ACKNOWLEDGMENTS

I thank my mom, Alice Mae Thompson, and my dad, the late Willie Dave Thompson Sr., for giving me life. To my wonderful husband, David Lee Goffney Jr., and my four beautiful daughters, Santavia A. Cole, Sanshae T. Goffney, Shani'ya L. Goffney, and Shantel S. Goffney. Thank you all for allowing me the opportunity to complete this outstanding achievement in my life. Without you, I would not be the woman I am today. Santavia is married to my handsome son-in-law Jarvis Cole Sr. Their children are my four amazing grandbabies, Jarvis Jr., Shanyira, S'Kiya, and Selah. I love being their glam-ma. Relatives and friends thank you immensely for your work behind the scenes. I could not have done it without you. A special thanks to my college tutor, who encouraged me in the beginning. Mrs. P., I will miss you, RIP.

A superior THANK YOU to Mrs. Diretha Flemming. Without your constant push, there would be no document. Consistently, and I mean consistently every year, you asked me if I was writing my book. Words cannot express how I appreciate the push and what you saw in me. I realize the inspiration you gave is the same I must give to other women. I hope this book inspires others to do just that. You didn't give up on me. You saw greatness I didn't see in myself, and for that, I am grateful. You taught me that consistency is not always what we think it is, but it's how long it takes for the person to see what you see in them.

To my photographers, editors, graphic designer, and publisher, *All In One Woman* would not be the book it is without your assistance.

Thank you immensely for your diligence behind the scenes.

Thank you, church family, God's Restoration Revival Center Holiness Church, for your love and support.

I thank my siblings, my sissy, Forever Friend, and my in-laws, my aunties, uncles, and extended family, sisters-in-law, brothers-in-law, nieces, nephews, cousins, extended friends, co-workers, business associates, churches, and prayer partners for staying by my side through the good, the bad, and the ugly.

FOREWORD

When Roberta asked me to write her foreword, I was honored, but I also suggested she ask other people instead. However, she firmly said, "No, I want you to write it." I do have to say it was an easy assignment to write. The reason it was easy is because of the life Roberta lives. The first thing that came to mind was Proverbs 31:10-31.

Yes, Roberta is the modern-day virtuous woman. She is a faithful and loving wife to her husband. She is a teacher and role model to her daughters. She wakes up early in the morning and makes sure her family has wholesome meals to eat and her home is running smoothly before she goes out and tackles her business affairs.

Roberta is most definitely a businesswoman by heart. She is a goal-driven go-getter, and she's caring and helpful to everybody. I truly admire her Christ-like lifestyle. Not only is Roberta a friend, but she is an awesome business associate. Our conversations are always positive.

She is one of the most positive people I have ever met. Roberta always wears a beautiful smile along with her pleasing personality.

Thank you, Roberta, Mrs. CEO, for your unconditional friendship, and most of all, congratulations on your first book. YOU DID IT!!!!

Diretha Flemming

INTRODUCTION

In 1992, at nineteen years old, I worked my first job at Dairy Queen. That moment I realized I didn't want to work for someone else all my life. I stood bold, and I meant what I said standing in the middle of the dining room, "I don't want to work for anybody else all my life!" As life took its course, I went with the flow. In 1999, only seven years later, God set me up according to my heart's desire, and I missed it. Fast-forward to 2001, my husband wanted me to stay home and raise our children. I missed it again. I let distractions and imbalance send me to the workplace instead of sharpening what I already had. All I had to do was worship God, take care of my husband and small children, manage what we had, and excel. But I made it more challenging than it had to be.

I pray this short story is as therapeutic for you as it was for me. Several times, I had to say, "Ouch," which made me better and helped me grow stronger.

God revealed how it was supposed to be, but that's not how it turned out. But because of my pure heart, God was patient and gave me a chance to "just be." Take a glimpse of my life's journey with me and see for yourself.

CHAPTER 1
The Girl Before the Woman

"Get out that mirror, gal. Come in this kitchen and wash your hands so we can eat supper. Call your sisters and brothers from outside."

While walking away from the mirror, "Mom, do you want me to wash my hands first or get my sisters and brothers?"

"Watch your mouth, Shelett! And do what I told you. You know what I mean." Murmuring, I ran outside for my siblings. Priscilla, the oldest daughter; Alicia, the next-to-the-oldest girl; Theortis, the oldest brother; our baby sister Mona Lisa; and our baby brother, Willie Dave Thompson Jr. Altogether, there were six of us. How in the world did they do it, deliver hundreds of babies? Just kidding, but it sure did seem like it in the early '70s. After doing what mom told me,

I walked into the kitchen to wash my hands. Back then, we had no inside restroom, so the only place I could wash my hands was the kitchen sink.

Oh wait! Let me tell you how my journey began. August 16, 1972, Willie Dave Thompson Sr. and Alice Mae (Williams) Thompson had their second baby, this time a girl. They named her Roberta Shelett Thompson. The middle child on my mom's side and the oldest daughter for my dad. My mom and dad separated when I was about six years old; she moved us into my grandparents' house.

I loved living with my grandparents, but I sure did miss my daddy.

"Cock-a-doodle-doo!" Gosh, I cherished that sound. Anytime I heard the rooster crow, I sensed it was early in the morning. When I looked out the screen door and saw my grandmother, Dorothy, alone, that was my chance to spend time with her. She sat on the porch in an old rocking chair, sipping her coffee. I walked outside to join her. She raised her head from the porch and smiled. Her beautiful gold teeth shined, her high chocolate cheeks glowed, and we exchanged our good mornings. I sat beside my granny in the empty rocker. I guess the look in my eyes spoke for me. Granny smiled and discerned that I was grateful for being in her presence.

"You want a sip?"

With a nod and the words to follow, "Yes, ma'am," I drank the bit of coffee in awe.

Granny stared, looking across the street. "Baby, you never walk out of your house all fixed up and your house dirty. And never forget, understanding beats the world." My grandmother and I didn't have a lot of time together, but she always had something wise to say when we did. Of the many things she told me, these two phrases stuck. There were other times I desired to talk to my grandma, but someone would always be in her presence.

The same with my grandpa, Henry Sr. When my baby sister and I had the opportunity to visit with Papa, he always told jokes and rhymes. He made me feel like the most precious, appreciated granddaughter in the world. He sang and rhymed all at once, "Corn grows tall, cotton thick, the way I love you baby make the old folks sick." Oh boy! The world couldn't tell me nothing; my papa *loved* me.

"Tell me another one, Papa, please! Tell me another one." He did.

My mom didn't want us tiring Papa out. He was bedridden and sometimes ill. So after about an hour, she would call us to wash up for dinner. "Good night, Papa, we love you." Tall and slender, lying in bed, Papa would wave goodnight. Looking through my youthful eyes, he looked like a giant. I couldn't understand why his feet hung over the mattress in the king-size bed. I learned later that papa was part Indian.

As usual, my mom poured our bath water into an old foot tub she had for us girls. The foot tub sat in the bedroom where my sisters and I slept. I remembered her making about three trips to the bedroom, carrying a big pot, yelling, "Stay out of the way, this water is hot!" We'd take a bath and go to bed.

When I visited my dad's mom, the situation was the same. My grandmother, Evelyn, always had someone in her presence. But I enjoyed every chance I got with her. Grandma Evelyn had beautiful shiny material in every room, and she used some of it for her quilts. One day, I picked up a piece of cloth, tossed it over my shoulder, and like a big shot, strutted across her bedroom floor. "Grandma, when I become rich, I'm going to buy you a house."

She glanced at me and smiled, "Oh, Granny would love that." I loved Granny Evelyn for as long as I could. Unfortunately, when night fell, all us children had to walk back to Granny Dorothy and Papa Henry's house, a.k.a. Plutie.

I thought the road home was the darkest road ever, with minimal lighting. The bats flew low, and being somewhat scared of the wild, I ducked. The bats spooked me, and my oldest brother didn't make things any better. We didn't go to church much, but I knew to call on the Lord, especially since my brother had me thinking the bats sucked the blood from humans' necks.

Once we'd get into the house, I'd be more than relieved, especially after walking the Hole's long dark road. "The Hole" was a country road with many wooded acres and little to no lighting, plus the neighbors were a few wooded acres away. We were actually supposed to get home before dark anyway, before the streetlights came on, or we'd be in trouble. That was a rule I could agree with.

Although my siblings and I lived with our grandparents, I thought we had it relatively good as children. Growing up, we'd wring the water out of our clothes after they washed them with a handheld rotator, take the clothes to the clothesline, and hang them up with clothespins as part of our everyday life. We'd also pack hot water from the kitchen to the foot tub to take a bath at night. This may not sound like having it good, but it was my life, and I was fine. I had my family and my big imagination; I was not worried about a thing until I went to school.

There, I learned quickly. Although what I didn't comprehend before didn't hurt me, classmates brought questions to my attention, causing me to review my life.

"Roberta, what did you do this weekend? Where are you going for Spring Break? Where are you going for summer break?"

"Wait. Did I miss something?"

My classmates' parents were still together, and it disappointed me how marriage challenges separated my parents. Now that did hurt. My peers' conversations were a lot different than mine. I had more family, but they had more stuff. I also lacked my mom, dad, sisters, and brothers all under one roof: a family. I tried not to think about my mates' comments. They were entitled to their opinion. Besides, their remarks stretched my brain to wander; I needed the nudge. After arriving home, I didn't dwell on school conversation; I enjoyed the evening with family and respected our life.

Every now and then on weekends, I got to look at wrestling when the grown folks were not talking in the living room. When the adults occupied the front room, it was a no-no for children to be in grown folks' business. I remember one Saturday in particular; Junkyard Dog was on TV. The house roared for Junkyard Dog! "Another One Bites The Dust," his theme song, rocked. "Another one bites the dust, hey, hey." Talk about fun times! That kind of excitement lasted all day for us kids as we ran outside still singing.

On another beautiful day around 1979, the wind breezed and it felt like spring, not too hot, not too cold. The weather was just right. I stood on the paved road all by myself, not sure where the other kids hid.

The sky's colors spoke volumes. After admiring the fluffy clouds and the blue background, I declared, "I know I'm going to heaven." The sky appeared indescribably beautiful and so full of peace. What a day to remember; the peace indicated how life was supposed to be.

"Children, come wash your hands and eat!" My petite mother interrupted my deep thought.

"Yes, Mama!" I ran inside. I couldn't help but reflect on the blue sky and sunshine.

Life carried on. Birthday parties were limited because there were so many of us. However, I distinctly remember one pleasant summer morning, on August 16, 1982, everyone sang "Happy Birthday" to me. Oh my, what a way to wake up! I was turning ten years old, and my family decorated with the little they had. I blushed nonstop. All this for me?

As usual, the children all ran outside to play, but the beautiful aroma of the birthday cake was so enticing. I snuck in silently, thinking to myself, "How much longer before we celebrate?" Tick-tock, the clock moved so slowly. "Come on, three o'clock. Let's party!" Just when I couldn't take it any longer, a voice called, "Children, come wash up." Yeah!

We all gathered in the kitchen. What a crowd. My eyes sparkled, my cheeks blushed, and my family loved on me liked I'd never experienced. This celebration was the happiest day of my life, all about me, and it was because of my auntie. With a big hug around her waist and tears in my eyes, I thanked her immensely. "Thank you, Auntie. I've never had a birthday party!"

With pure love in her eyes, she said, "Oh, Brown Sugar, auntie wanted to do this for you, and I love you too." I smiled with great appreciation.

In the early eighties, nothing was cheap. Microwave ovens were around $400 and up.

Unlike that birthday, our Christmases were usually meager. We received apples, oranges, and pecans, not flashy presents like our classmates, but we tried to be grateful. One Christmas, however, we performed so poorly, my mom said, "If y'all don't stop that mess, I'm gone show you better than I can tell you." We understood perfectly what that meant—a butt whipping. We didn't want that for Christmas, so we mustered up some appreciation.

However, one aunt bought us all a real present. When I unwrapped mine, it was . . . a cracker box? Grateful me said, "Thank you, Auntie."

She snickered, "Open the gift!"

"Oh, you got me, Auntie." Inside laid a cute pink wristwatch. I squeezed my aunt and ran away with my new toy.

Many of our older aunties did what they could for us. On my mother's side was: Aunt Bertha, Ella, Christine, and Kimmie. On my father's side was: Aunt Mable, Iva, Irene, and Mary. I've always been so appreciative of them.

My uncles on my mom's side were: Henry Jr. and Albert. On my dad's side was: Uncle Jerry, Donald, Terry Earl, Tommy, Walter, Edward, and Alvin Jr.

But there was one special Christmas I'd never forget. My family knew how I loved to play school, so my mom bought me a chalkboard. I never had to leave the house again. I had my chalkboard and a real eraser; that was the happiest day of my life. Until one dreadful day, my board disappeared. I searched high and low, no chalkboard. I asked my family members if anyone had seen it.

One mumbled, "Theortis had it. He made a roof for his dog's house."

"What! How could he do that? Why would he do that?" Now that hurt. I was so mad at him! I wanted to wring his neck! Could I wring his neck? I stormed out the door looking for him. There he was, working on his doghouse, across the street.

"Why did you tear my chalkboard up for your dog?

Why would you do that to me!"

"Awe, girl, don't come here with all that crying. You weren't playing with it."

"Yes I was, Thee. I had schoolwork to finish."

"Girl, gone with that."

"You old punk!"

"Girl, I'ma show you a . . ."

Mama stormed out of the house with a strap in her hand. "Y'all stop that mess right now! What's gotten into you? Don't neither one of you say a mumbling word. I don't care who started it; you're both wrong. Brothers and sisters shouldn't act like that. Now hug and kiss on the cheek and make up."

Oh Lord. My mama believed hugging and kissing was the quickest way to forgive. With tears in my eyes and stubborn as a mule, and a frown on his face, we hugged and kissed on the cheek. Yuck! After a few days of mourning, I did what I usually do: I sucked it up and kept it moving.

As time moved on, one auntie came home to visit from a different state. This time the children were not allowed in the living room where the adults gathered. The grown folk laughed and cut up so much, I wanted to see what was going on! I eased the door open just enough to look through the crack with one eye. My God, what a woman, her appearance was breathtaking. She dressed in a charming white mink coat, her hair combed perfectly. She wore long, shiny red nails, her face was polished nicely, and she set it off with a soft yet noticeable lipstick. Yep, I thought to myself, my future—black and beautiful!

Time rocked on, and my life took a turn. I had a horrible experience I wouldn't want any little girl to encounter. Excruciating, to say, someone molested me. The molester pulled me in the room, yanked my shirt up, and sucked my breast. I could not believe this happened! He said, "If you tell, no one will believe you with your hot self." I was hurt, scared, young, and confused. I wanted to tell my mom, but how? I couldn't tell my grandpa. All he talked about was shooting somebody if they harmed his family. It would have been my fault if my papa killed someone because of my confession. I held it in. *Who do I trust? What will this do to the rest of my family? Is it going to be my fault because I'm "hot?"* I cried, forgave, and realized I had to keep going. The wound changed my world; it fogged my big imagination. My attitude became evil after that tragic experience. I never stopped believing in God, but I lost faith in men. I called him a name beyond *child molester*. A real man didn't touch little girls. If another *** put his hands on me, he would pay, and I meant *literally*. With that said, I toughened up and left the past in the past.

Eventually, my mom got an apartment—whoo-hoo!—and I finally witnessed how my friends at school lived.

It was pleasant, but where was my family? It seemed like life scattered everyone. No doubt, the apartment was nice, but family fellowship meant more to me. Granny and Papa weren't there. I didn't see my aunties and genuine uncles much. The good old days looked dim. At times mama left, but she couldn't be far, considering she couldn't drive. If she needed an item from the store, she had to catch a ride there and back.

Somedays, I played school all by myself. Although my horrible experience had fogged my big imagination, I never stopped being the teacher. I took a brown flat beer box, opened all four corners, and tacked it to the wall since my brother destroyed my chalkboard. For my eraser, I used toilet tissue. The old *TV Guides* were my teacher's book, and I had my students go through and circle every word with a specific letter in it. For example, the word *me* had the letter *m*, so my make-believe students (stuffed animals) or sometimes my siblings had to read through the *TV Guide* and circle all the words that began with the letter *m*.

My brother asked, "Are you still in here playing school, girl?"

"Yes, come play with me."

"Oh no!" he said with his nose stuck in the air. "You play school *too long*!"

I brushed him off. When he got bored, he'd play.

"If you keep using that tissue for an eraser, you're going to be using newspaper to handle your business." Yep, that was Mama. I couldn't explain how much I loved it.

As the hours rushed by, like any other Sunday night, we put our entertainment away and prepped for school the next day. Around this time of the year, girls tried out for cheerleading. My classmates pumped me up. "Try out, Roberta! We will vote for you; you will be a great cheerleader." I knew my friends were right. I loved to jump, do splits, and yell, and I was going to try out.

That afternoon on the way home from school, I was so excited, but the bus driver drove slower than a turtle. "Hurry up," I thought to myself. "I have some great news for my mama." Once, I made it home, just like any other school day, our supper was prepared, sitting on the stovetop, and our house was clean.

I rushed to tell her, but she tried telling me what she cooked. Her news didn't excite me as much as my great news boiled down on the inside, waiting to explode like a volcano. I finally got my chance! I told her as if we won the lottery. She stared into my eyes and placed her hands on my shoulders. "Baby, Mama can't afford for you to be a cheerleader." It felt like I had received the news that someone had died. She explained, "Camp is over $1,000, and I'm not sure what else you will need."

"Well, my oldest sister was a cheerleader."

My mom and I talked for an hour about me being a cheerleader. She expressed how my sister's dad paid every penny for her to participate. I asked, "Why can't he help you pay for me, maybe give half or something?" I never understood people back then and their justifications. If you give to one child, give to the other children. I had no idea about child support and how all that worked. She tried, but she couldn't make me understand. The behavior from the grown-ups around me confused me even more. People were drinking, smoking, gambling, partying, and having a good time. Didn't that cost money? But I couldn't be a cheerleader? Was the kid confused or the grown folk(s) confused?

I didn't verbally ask it, but I bet my face did. Unfortunately, I didn't try out to be a cheerleader. It crushed me like many things destroyed me growing up. My big imagination got dimmer. I took it like a big girl and, in time, healed.

CHAPTER 2

Runaway

Just when I thought things were getting better, our family experienced a major heartbreak. May of 1988 I was a few months shy of turning sixteen when a car hit my baby brother. Willie Dave Thompson Jr. was riding his bicycle to the store with his friend. The incident brought devastation to my family. When I received the news, it numbed me. I couldn't believe it. The ambulance rushed him to the hospital, but sad to say, he didn't survive. After that tragedy, my mom changed tremendously. The disaster affected our entire family. I understood little of what went on as a teenager. I had my past that I was battling, along with losing my baby brother. Within months, mine and my mom's relationship turned into tit for tat.

One day we got into the biggest argument, and she turned as if she could have wrung my neck like a chicken and said with great force, "Roberta Shelett! It's not what you say, it's how you say it! It's not what you do, it's how you do it!" I froze. I didn't say another word to my mother, but my tongue of facts and truths were no longer welcomed. She terrified me when she threatened to put me in the girl's home. I wasn't that "bad." I just couldn't express myself without being disrespectful, rude, or straightforward.

I ran to my grandmother Evelyn's house. I cried and told her the time had come for me to run away. I was hurt, angry, frustrated, confused, all but "Sweet 16." I explained that I needed someone to trust. This mess all happened within six months of my brother dying.

I had no idea where I was going or who I would be staying with, but I didn't want to be a burden for my mother.

I hung out with a female friend, and from her house, I hopped from place to place, never turning back. This encounter lasted for about a year until I dated an older man, my sugar daddy. The relationship was bittersweet. He took care of me, and I experienced safety and freedom. I had so much money in my pocket, the reality of him being a lot older than me was irrelevant. In those days, $60–

$100 a week was a lot of money for a girl my age. When my girlfriends and I went to the liquor store, I picked up the tab. I was Ms. Bigshot: "Please, let me."

I balled and *not* on a budget. You couldn't tell me nothing.

I loved a good time. We sipped Strawberry Hill, Budweiser, Schlitz Malt Liquor Bull; you name it, I drank it. But my pick of all was Schlitz Malt Liquor Bull. I met new friends; we smoked marijuana and partied every chance we got. Yep, living the *good life*!

When my funds got low, I'd asked my sugar daddy, "How was your day?" Looking like he'd had a rough one, "Fine."

"Well, how are your kinfolks doing?"

He stared at me with a suspicious look on his face, "Who?"

"Grant, Jackson, Hamilton, and Jefferson," I said.

"Shelett, who is that?"

"Those dead presidents in your pocket."

"Girl, you know how to get what you want!" We giggled the rest of the evening and enjoyed the humorous moment. When night fell, my girlfriends and I reunited.

One summer day, my sugar daddy and I had a heart

to heart. Fortunately, our communication helped both of us. He insisted that I quit bouncing around from place to place and become his assistant. He understood my firm tongue and straightforwardness, and the chat helped me be a better person. Finally, someone understood me. I danced!

"You have to get your GED, Shelett," he explained. "Your lifestyle can't survive on minimum wage." Back in those days, minimum wage was $4.25 an hour.

"Wait. No more parties?"

He said parties needed to be limited. I took his advice and studied for the GED test and failed the first time. A test was the last thing on my mind. If someone yelled party, they had my attention. I studied nonstop the second time around. I could barely focus, but I passed.

My achievement deserved a reward, but instead of partying, I kept my focus on my education. One of my good friends helped me complete the paperwork for enrollment at Angelina College. It looked like I was on the right road and was going to be a grade-school teacher—or so I thought.

One day, my girlfriend, who I had been riding with to college, told me about her new job position and that she wouldn't be able to drive back and forth—another heartbreaker, eighteen years old and stranded. I envisioned getting a job in my hometown and paying someone to drive me to Lufkin then back to Corrigan. Great idea, but it didn't quite work out that way.

I started partying and drinking again. One night we had a house party at one of my guy friends' houses. We were having a good time until suddenly someone uninvited showed up. "What she show up for? Everybody out!" I said.

A short little chic, one who I didn't like and who didn't like me, walked up to me, rolled her neck, and said, "Hasta la vista, baby."

By that time, I felt like Junkyard Dog's little sister . . . BAM! I hit her dead in her face. My girlfriend shouted, "OH, NO! DON'T FIGHT IN THE HOUSE! NO, NOT IN THE HOUSE!" Someone threw us out on the wet porch, in the rain. I slipped, and all I remember was trying to hold on to her throat. She bit my fingers, somehow on my left hand, causing them to swell. I was drunk as a skunk that night.

The next day several folks said, "That girl wanted to kill you."

"Why? We both were drunk! We looked like fools in

the rain fighting because we had too much alcohol and marijuana in our system. But tell her to come on. There's nothing between us besides air and opportunity! And remind her, don't dis' it if she can't take it." I realized I didn't want that to be my character.

It was a blessing I/we didn't go to jail. I had to make better decisions. Looking over my shoulders every few seconds because I whipped someone's behind, or they whipped mine was not an option for me. Watching others, listening, and reflecting, I knew this was not the life for me.

A couple of months later, I met a new friend and visited another city. I applied for a job. The guy I dated knew a lady, who described me to her supervisor. The manager called me in for an interview. I was so nervous. Once the interview started and ended, we sat across from each other laughing and talking.

Guess what? I got the job! In 1991, minimum wage was $4.25 an hour.

In the beginning, I struggled with the rotation in the restaurant. I was not good in the kitchen and horrible at breaking down the ice cream machine. I could tell

I was on thin ice. The shift manager approached me and said, "The supervisor is giving you a certain amount of time, and after that, she's anticipating letting you go." The sweet lady took me under her wing and showed me the ropes. My training took one night in every area with her, and I mastered the setup. My performance pleased the supervisor. After that, work was excellent! But my boyfriend and I were not so great.

I didn't want to quit my job, but the relationship I was in was over. My boyfriend's actions indicated I didn't need any more writing on the wall, and I didn't ignore the truth. If a buddy doesn't want me, just say so.

The truth is, he wanted me and the alcohol. He drank so much, every time I looked around it seemed like dusk 'til dawn. Once it was so bad, I had to drive him home; I dared not jeopardize my life riding with a drunk driver. When I tried to talk to him about drinking, that caused a dreadful argument. As calmly as I could, with a firm face, I reminded him, "Don't do anything you might regret." The night settled, and we went to bed.

The next day my girlfriend picked me up to visit my

sugar daddy, who was now more like a good friend.

We had a heart-to-heart. He was proud of me, happy that I was doing well on my new job, but he insisted I go back to college. I felt obligated to my occupation, customers, and coworkers. I had another extended family, and I couldn't quit my position. This employment was my first ever. I explained I would save some money and would go back to college when time permitted.

He gave me his blessings and helped me buy my first car. It was a four-door Ford Tempo. I told him, "This car does not look like me."

He asked, "You don't think fat meat greasy, do you? This is what you can afford. Now drive the vehicle or leave it parked." I took the keys. I didn't appreciate what I had. I thought the car was ugly and for a fifty-year-old woman. I was nineteen! I didn't want a four-door car looking like an old lady.

I swallowed my pride, especially since he had been right about everything else he had told me. The next day I went to work. "Oh, you got a new ride, I see. How can you afford that?" asked my coworker.

"Excuse me?" Now, remember, I thought the Tempo was old-fashioned and ugly. My notes were only $150 a month. I had no bills, and I worked twenty-five to twenty-nine hours a week. And you better believe if this fashionista had a boyfriend, he helped if I needed support.

Back then, several called me a gold digger. I didn't care. I couldn't understand how some were a "broke" digger but not a "gold" digger? Several women worked, paid all the bills, and had a man stretched out on her couch. Naw . . . I wasn't the confused one. Anyway, I didn't say that out loud, but you better believe the thought crossed my mind. I smiled, shook my head, and prepped for work. From there, I drove back and forth from city to city. Then, one day, my boyfriend showed up.

He asked if I was free later when I got off from work. I told him, "Free? No, but I'll be reasonable." He had acted a fool a few nights before. "No, I'm not free all night for you, knucklehead. But I will give you a reasonable amount of time to apologize." He needed to apologize. One night he had been drinking, and I believed in protecting my body. He liked to drink, and there's no telling what else he might have done. I didn't play like that.

We were smooching, embracing one another, and I

said, "Grab the raincoat (condom)."

Knucklehead said, "Not tonight."

What did he say that for?

"Naw. You get the raincoat!"

Remember, this was a conversation going on while we were kissing. Somewhat of a tussle began. Now with more firmness in my voice, I told him, "You are NOT freaking me without a condom!" I had a flashback. I had made myself a promise. No man would take advantage of me without me getting revenge. HIV and AIDS were spreading like wildfire.

I had a flashback of my uncle talking to one of his friends. (He didn't realize I listened while lighting him a cigarette.) "You can kill the crabs with Blue Star Ointment, but it won't cure AIDS."

I was determined to stay healthy. "If you want some goody, the only way you're going to get it is to use protection!" BAM! I socked him. It hurt me more than it hurt him, but I meant what I said. "Now, are you going to use protection?" He curled over, holding his privates, grunting. Yes, I deserved that apology. That's *not* how you treat a lady, at least not this one.

The next day, he apologized and said he had made a mistake. Of course, I gave him another chance.

Time progressed. My relationship was good, work was good, and I was good. This is how it was supposed to be, everything perfect.

Until one unforgettable day, our supervisor snapped. I tried everything in my power to stay out of her way. She stood in front of the entire restaurant of people and screamed at me. Oh boy, before I knew it, I was saying, "You better watch who you are screaming at in front of all these folks."

"Roberta, in the BACK!"

"I SURE WILL!"

We stomped to her office, and the dispute exploded. "Lesson one, Supervisor, you need to learn how and when to talk to folks. I have what it takes to go anywhere I want to go. I'm never working for anyone all my life!" She said what she had to say and vice versa. The disagreement went on and on. Finally, the dust settled; she apologized, and in return, so did I. I returned to my duty post, and from that day forward, our relationship bloomed.

As time passed on, my boyfriend loved that alcohol more than he did me. In the game of dating, I didn't tolerate several behaviors in a man too long. That bull crap got old. Dating, in my world, meant he fit my criteria and I fit his. All we could do was try. If the writing was on the wall, as the old folks say, don't ignore it.

After about a year and a half, my attitude changed, "If it doesn't fit, don't force it; just relax and let him go." There are more fish in the sea. So, if my boyfriend cheated, abused alcohol or drugs, or was a mental or physical abuser, what was to work out? I had a mirror; somebody wanted me. Speaking of a mirror, I didn't fall for pretty boys who loved the mirror more than I did. I knew if he were a high-yellow, "hey good looking, what you got cooking tonight" type, I would never be enough for him. With that said, I left my heart at the house and enjoyed the date.

Anyhow, I decided that evening, when I got off work, that I was going back to Corrigan and driving back and forth until I could go back to college. I had a flashback and had to be wise about the actions I took, considering I had left one night and my boyfriend had come after me with a knife. My sugar daddy would have never done anything like that. Anyway, my boyfriend and I landed in a ditch and tussled. He had me in a position and said, "B, if you leave me tonight, I swear I'm going to KILL YOU!" With the knife against my throat, I got up, drenched in sticky mud, and drove him home. One thing he taught me, if nothing else, is a drunk man will tell a sober man's story. I learned my lesson fooling with this jealous old man. If I left my mama's house at sixteen, leaving him would save my life, but if I stayed, one of us wouldn't survive. As time passed, I kept my distance and remained a respectful friend.

Work progressed, and he stopped by my job to borrow my car one day to run and pick up a part he needed to fix his car. After that last episode, I wondered if I should let him borrow my car or not. I figured it was 10:00 a.m.—he'd be back before my shift ended. So, I let him borrow the vehicle. In my head, I had my escape all planned out. Since I let him borrow my car, that would keep our relationship on a "friendship" level. He had no idea I planned to go back to my hometown that night and never come around again. Tick-tock went the clock. He was a no-show. My shift was going to end in about an hour, and in 1992, Knucklehead didn't have a cell phone. I prayed he had not been drinking in my car and gotten pulled over.

A girlfriend I worked with took me to her house. By this time, I was livid. We tried playing spades to distract my mind from the situation, but it didn't work. Playing a card game was the last thing on my mind. My stomach knotted up. I didn't know how to feel or think or what to believe. My friend took me back to his house—still a no-show. I walked to his mom's house; I guess the look on my face spoke for me. She said, "Baby, it will be alright. Have a seat and look at the news with me. He'll be back soon." In my mind, the heck it would be all right: this BLEEPITY BLEEP HAD MY CAR! I had better synonyms than heck and bleepity bleep.

Two days passed. By midday of day three, the cops were at Mr.'s house when he got home. I was so mad! He had pissed me off beyond being pissed off! He'd *never* be able to say another word to me. The female officer caught me by my left arm, gently turned me away, and said, "He's not worth it. Keep walking; take a deep breath. Once they remove him from your car and search it, you can go." So much was racing through my mind. Lord, please let no drugs or opened bottles of alcohol be in my car. The male officer ordered us to come back to the car; I got in my car that smelled like alcohol, cigarettes, and whatever else you can imagine.

As I drove off, I realized revenge I couldn't conquer, tears flowed down my face. I sucked it up like a big girl. The best way to forget about him was to date another one, and I moved on. That night I went back to my ex-sugar daddy's house, who was more of my guidance during this time. I told him a little about what happened. He stayed consistent. "It is time for you to go back to college, Shelett."

I told him, "You keep saying that, but you have your own business and your house paid for, and you own a lot of land. It looks like you are doing fine."

He stated, "But it was a lot of hard work. You are a smart girl, and for the things you like, you will need to go to college." He was right. Or was he? I had "champagne taste on a beer budget." We finished the conversation, and I promised I'd finish school.

I took a couple of days off to let things cool down. I didn't want to lay eyes on that jive turkey, but my coworkers needed me. Therefore, I went back to work, but on this day an army convoy stopped by. Oh, wee. All the girls cheesed from ear to ear. Look what's coming through the door. Yep, I just got over old boy.

Tall, dark, and handsome. Yes, please, I will take one on the rocks. I took the orders of each customer. After I carried out the food, I met my new friend. I didn't realize he was a setup to help change my life from turning back to drinking alcohol and smoking weed. When we dated, he educated me on Army Seals. Honestly, I wasn't listening to a word he said. That conversation bored the stuffing out of me. I wanted to party; the dance floor called my name. It seemed like the weekends I had off, he showed up at my apartment. Did he see the schedule before I did? It seemed like it.

CHAPTER 3
The Drug Bust

One particular weekend my new boyfriend didn't come to town. Whoo-hoo! I was so excited! My girlfriends and I were going to PARTYYY! There was nothing like a girls' night out.

Every chance I got, I danced!

This day I had a little free time on my hands, so before going to my girlfriend's house to finish getting ready, I stopped by our mutual friend's apartment. You know, just checking in. Well, our mutual buddy wasn't home, but before I left, I asked the owner, "Sir, may I use the ladies' room?"

"It's down the hall to your left," he said.

My cheerful self told him, "Thank you."

BAM! "Police!"

"Police?" I yanked my britches up! I touched the window blinds. Naw, I better not climb out the window. If a cop is outside, I'll get shot. BAM! The restroom door flew open.

"Hands up!"

I obeyed. My heart raced a thousand miles per hour; everything happened so fast. The female officer snatched me around. "Hands behind your head!" She frisked me. Tears formed. I felt so ashamed. What in the world was going on?! I dared not to ask her that, but curiosity was killing the cat. All I did was listen and did what she told me to do. After the pat down, she ordered me to turn around. "I have to check to make sure you don't have any drugs on you," she said.

"Yes, ma'am." She had me raise my bra and drop my britches.

"UGHHH!!! Is this happening to me?" I thought.

She looked at me, "What are you doing here?" I didn't say a mumbling word. The look in her eyes expressed how much she cared. "If we find no drugs, you can go." Thoughts raced through my mind and tears rolled down my face. I realized I was at the wrong place at the wrong time.

My mom and I hadn't talked in a while, but I could hear her voice, "Quit pissing at everybody's house! You should have held that piss till later!"

An hour rolled by, and we were still sitting there. By this time, the female officer and I walked outside so they could search the restroom more in-depth. I prayed silently, "Lord, please don't let them find any drugs in this apartment. You know I'm innocent. I was just checking on my friend. Drugs are overrated anyway, and why in the world were the cops at this house? Maybe that's why he's not here, hmm . . ." Although the episode was shameful, it gave me a lot of time to reminisce. Hard drugs were never a thing of mine. A little "Mary Jane" every weekend, maybe. The other stuff, like shooting needles in my arms or smoking crack was never an option for me. Oh, some folks offered it to me, but I couldn't understand why some would do such a drug that caused them to lose it all. No thank you.

My girlfriends probably were worried sick. Cars drove by, and the people inside stared. The cops stopped the vehicles and looked inside. Goodness, it was so embarrassing. I hoped no one told my mother. I cared less about what anyone else thought, but my mom didn't need any worries.

"You are free to go."

"Thank you, Jesus. I've got to be more careful!"

Although that was an embarrassing experience, I realized it could have been worse—a night or two in jail and maybe even a narcotic charge. Nevertheless, God protected me.

CHAPTER 4

The Woman

My new boyfriend portrayed himself as a gentleman at first, but I learned the root of him not long afterward. Our dates became slim. I tiptoed around nauseated often and didn't know why. The months passed. I began to worry. HOW IN THE WORLD DID I LET THAT SLIP UP ON ME? What in the world was I thinking? I have always tried to take care of myself, and I slipped? I told my childhood friend what happened, and she encouraged me. She told me not to worry; she had my back. I went to the doctor after giving it some time. He said, "I got your test results. You are fine. You have nothing to worry about." I shouted and cried! I not only wanted to be healthy for myself, but I was a twenty-one-year-old trying to find myself, and the last thing I wanted to do was bring a child into the world unhealthy. Mr. Convoy wasn't around as much; he always traveled. Perpetrating to be pure, he looked at me one of the last times I saw him and said, "If you never see me again, realize I love you."

In my mind, I was like, "Dude, I'm a street girl! I understand what you are saying. You lied about your other relationship, and now you can't tell me the truth. I get it . . . Papa was a rolling stone. Wherever he laid his hat was home." I wanted to say that out loud so bad, but I didn't. The marijuana had not burned all my brain cells. Please! Give me a break. He was still lying, and I was still thinking: "It is not about you; it is about the hanky-panky." I asked the Lord to forgive me, and I didn't beat myself up about it. Disappointed? Absolutely, but I would not die from it.

On September 22, 1994, I had a beautiful, healthy baby girl and named her Santavia. From that day forward, the girl Roberta became a woman. I made a vow to myself that I would be the best mother I could be for her, and I strived to do that.

As time went on, I became a substitute teacher in my hometown and later became full time. I loved it. I spent a lot of time with my beautiful baby girl. But after a while, I had to decide, considering I just got my own apartment right before she was born and had little money. My girlfriend informed me that the Texas Department of Criminal Justice (TDCJ) was hiring, so we applied. We decided that job could help us profit. In those days, you had to wait until TDCJ called for employment.

Meanwhile, I pursued classes at Angelina College in Lufkin, Texas, and at night, I took a sign language class and received a certificate. During the day, I studied psychology. Low and behold, guess what? As the semester ended for college, TDCJ asked me to come work for them.

Before I took the job, I confirmed my babysitting arrangements considering I had to travel to Beeville, Texas for training. It wasn't difficult taking care of one daughter. I always had a family who loved to babysit Santavia. That said, I traveled for training and every weekend I came home.

Once the academy closed, a few of us trained at a general population unit. Talk about out of the ordinary. Other officers patted us down every day as we entered the unit. My first day, I thought, "What have I gotten myself into?" The racket scared the mess out of me. Doors! Doors! And in my mind, "Oh Lord, they're letting the inmates out. I hope I remember my defensive moves on these big jokers."

As time went on, work became a normal part of my life. My firmness gained me respect. The inmates' manners turned from disrespect to Boss Lady. I wore my riot baton on my hip with pride. With the consistent practice of my defensive tactic moves every night, I was ready. I wasn't working to befriend the inmates; I had a job to do. If they said something to make me curse them out, I did. I was *free*. Initially I was not ashamed of being a TDCJ officer. I needed the atmosphere. In the world with the civilians, I couldn't curse nor fight. I'd go to jail. But in this world: Thompson, suit up! My anxiety from the gas mask terrified me, but the adrenaline of putting a bad boy in his place . . . YES SIR! Let's gas him!

After training, the supervisors transferred several of us to Ad-Seg. This unit was empty. The sergeant assigned everyone different duty posts. I can keenly remember the sergeant sending me to the recreation yard. When I got out there, this short little lady stood over by herself, leaning on the recreation yard fence, trying to stay in the shade as much as possible. It was rather hot outside, considering it was July. I noticed from a distance she didn't want to be bothered. Me being me, I spoke. With my genuine smile and love, I softened her. In return, she conversed. From observation, she had little to say, but we had two hours together. There was no way I'd be able to sit in the hot sun and not converse.

"Girl, it sure is hot out here, isn't it?"

She replied, "Yes, it is."

"I hope they do not forget about us."

With energy and a beautiful smile, she said, "They better not!" We giggled, and our relationship started from there.

This lady was as sweet as pie, a tad bit on the shy side but found a genuine love for me. My sister for life I met at TDCJ in the recreation yard in 1997. We had no idea where our relationship was going.

As my TDCJ life began, I met so many wonderful people. One coworker said one day, "From your conversation. I have the best man for you, Thompson."

"Oh?" I responded.

"Yes, you should meet him one day," she said. "I

believe you two will be great for each other."

"I don't know. I've had enough boyfriends; I should chill for a while."

She said, "Don't you mess around and let him get away."

Let's be real for a moment. I was at TDCJ. Parties, parties, and more parties. I was not trying to settle down at this time. Men are jealous. They do not want you hanging out with your girlfriends, not to mention I had started the new job to save a lot of money. I wasn't trying to hear about a man at the moment. I wasn't ready. Besides, I had not been single in my life for six months. As soon as freedom rang, another one tried to be possessive—maybe later. You tell a guy you only want to be friends, and he makes sure he is in your face daily. No, that is not a friendship. He wants a commitment-ship.

I had a quick reminder of what I told God: "God, I do not want a man I cannot trust with my little girl. I don't want an abusive man, a cheater, or an emotional abuser. Lord, help me. I don't want to live this life forever." That night assured me that God had listened but didn't reveal it.

Back to reality, work continued. Somedays, that

friend and I didn't work together, but one day she asked me, "Are you ready to meet my friend?"

I responded with a smile, "Why are you so adamant about me meeting your friend?"

She smiled beautifully, despite the braces on her teeth. "You two will be perfect for each other," she said. My mind wandered. She described this guy as a gentleman. But . . .

There is no need for me to run him off if I never bring him close. "Girlfriend, I will keep you posted."

As time went on, she finally persuaded me to go on a date, but I had one last question for her: "If he is the this and that you're raving about, why is he single?"

She responded, "He's picky."

"Okay, picky," was my response, with an upside-down smile, nodding my head, bringing that frown back into a smile. She could tell I was curious. "Okay, girlfriend, I will go on a date with him, but I need to look at a picture first."

A couple of days later, she brought me a snapshot.

"Oh! Sookie! Sookie. Sissy, look at this mandingo!" Sissy was the little lady I met in the recreation yard almost a year ago. We were all working inside the control picket. The picture fed me a six-foot-four man, wearing a long-sleeve white button-down collared shirt and light brown pants, with bowlegs out of this world. The weights fed his arms well with an iron metal called *muscles*. Girlfriend, bring me the digits! We laughed, worked, and played all day. She gave him my picture and phone number, and that was the beginning of us.

CHAPTER 5
Mr. Mandigo

Goodness. It was about time I arrived—what a drive. On June 20, 1998, I pulled into the Boles parking lot in Coldspring, Texas, where I met my new friend, David Lee Goffney Jr. It had been a sizzling summer day. Shorter than five feet five, yet petite, I wore a pair of black shorts with a black-and-white zip shirt that flaunted a little reveal; I dressed to impress. I caught his eyes from the passenger window looking. Unsure what came over me, I trembled in my G-string and continued sitting in my car for a couple of more minutes. I wondered why he didn't come open the door. I took a deep breath and got out of my car. Switching like a girl would, I confidently walked to his passenger door, opened it, placed my left foot on the floorboard, and ushered the rest of my body into the car. Our eyes connected. We both spoke at almost the same time. His eyes said, "Gosh, she is beautiful." My eyes and my thoughts were, "Ooh wee, Mr. Mandingo!" (A quick memory from the women back in the day, a mandingo is tall, dark, handsome, and big all over.) I couldn't take it! I turned my head and looked down at the floor mat.

Yes, please. I will take this one on the mountain; a rock will not do. Those muscles: I couldn't wait to get my hands on 'em. They were bigger in person than my girlfriend showed me in the picture.

"I'm glad you made it safely, Ms. Thompson."

"Thank you, Mr. Goffney."

"You didn't tell me I had to drive across the world to see you."

Humor showered the atmosphere, and we moved on. He headed to Wyatt's Cafeteria in Conroe, Texas. While on our way to the restaurant, we talked as if we'd known each other forever. Once we arrived at our destination, this time, he ran and opened the door for me. Once we washed up and began eating, I went back every time he went back for seconds. He had a strange look on his face. I didn't let his facial expression bother me one bit. Besides, I sensed I was with my long-life friend. We enjoyed one another's company so much that a movie didn't cross my mind.

After we finished dinner, we headed to Candy Cane Park to talk. Oh yeah! Holding hands, snickering, giggling, blushing at the sweet words he promised as we walked the paved trail—what an evening to remember. The date tempted us so much we didn't want to leave the park. Unfortunately, every good thing must come to an end.

We headed back to Coldspring to pick up my car. A moment of silence for both of us as he drove. In my mind, I thought, can this be real? A sincere date? He kept it respectful. Any other guy would try to . . . let's just say . . . not on the first date. Once we arrived back in the Boles parking lot, he put his car in park, turned, and said, "Sorry about earlier today when I didn't open the door for you."

Blushing as if I forgot about it, I said, "No problem." Still not sure why he didn't, I brushed it off. He got out of the car; his bowlegs, waistline, and upper torso held my attention as he strolled to the passenger side to open the door for me. Portraying himself as a gentleman, he took my hand, and I got out of his white Mitsubishi Galant. We walked to my Gold Chevy Malibu. After I sat in the driver's seat, I cranked it and let the window down.

With his long Jack's cookie smile, he said, "Follow me." We drove and sat down at the rest area at the brick church on Highway 150. We chatted until 2:00 a.m. Much of what we talked about are secrets we need to keep. Let's say, hot flash.

"Thank you for a lovely evening, Mr. Goffney."

With a smack on the lips, he replied, "My pleasure, Miss Thompson."

"I don't want you on the road this late by yourself, lady. Let me show you a quicker way home." That's when I learned the back road, which leads to 59 North.

That night was one of the most beautiful times of my life; I went out with a real man, a gentleman, a MANDINGO! That one date led to many.

Approximately one week later, I met my wonderful future mother-in-law: quiet and sweet as honey, unlike my future father-in-law, who drilled me with questions.

"Am I in the army?"

At first, I wasn't aware of David's dad's humorous

behavior, but I enjoyed the moment. David Jr. rescued me by telling his dad we had to leave. He drove me around the city, and I met another future sister-in-law and her two cute little boys. She appeared tall yet slender, and her demeanor sparked like the private investigator. We chatted for a while, and after that pleasant visit, we continued riding around, meeting his family and friends. One aunt's and uncle's heart were as pure as his mom's and dad's. They accepted me with open arms. I met cousins and more cousins. And one of my favorite times of all is when I gained two grandmothers, Grandma Bertha Mae (Hughes) Lewis and Grandma Mittie Pearl Edmond. What a joyful time . . .

One month—I remember it like yesterday—we were at his house chilling and having a good time. Low and behold, BAM, BAM, there was a pound on the door. "Who in the world is that, David Jr.?"

"My brother and his wife."

Shuffling while fixing my pinned, curled hair, I let out, "Oh, shucks!"

David covered my loud mouth with his hand. "Shh, maybe they'll leave." We pretended we were not home, but the cars in the driveway gave us away.

BAM, BAM, BAM.

"David, you may want to answer the door."

And there I met my future sister-in-law and brother-in-law. She smiled, and the curiosity on her face said, "What took you two so long to answer the door?"

After David introduced us, we laughed and talked, and I gained more loving family.

Every date after that became more rather than less. David Jr. consistently said, and I quote, "You're going to be my wife." I would just blush, drop my head, and continued with whatever I was doing. One night, after I made it home, a bit of frustration came over me. His voice echoed, sounding like a broken record, "You're going to be my wife. You're going to be my wife. You're going to be my wife."

Silently, I thought, "Okay, already. I listened the first time, but, no, I'm not." Then I spoke into the atmosphere, "Dude, I'm not thinking about marriage! I'm having a good time. Can we please enjoy the moments?" I had lived my past, but he only knew it in part. I had a whole lot of residue. This man was not my usual type of fellow. His eyes would always say what his heart felt for me. I wasn't a "rolling stone," but I didn't want folks telling him wherever I laid my head was my home. The last thing I wanted to do was hurt him. His kindness and patience had a hold on me. I let life happen and enjoyed the time.

One day after work, he was waiting for me at my house. I rarely invited him over since this old girl enjoyed a drink from time to time. He was so different, and I respected him to the core. There were just some things about me I didn't want him to know. And the fact that I could drink like a fish swam was one of them. Anyhow, he was there waiting. It had been a TDCJ meltdown day, and I needed a drink. I looked in the refrigerator, and most of my Budweisers were gone.

"Oh, wait a minute, David Jr., what happened to my beer in the fridge?"

He looked like he had seen a ghost. He fiddled with his fingers and stared at the TV.

I paused, then continued, "I need a drink."

His innocent eyes looked at me. "I gave them away." His pureness didn't make me emotional that day; I went fuming.

"Don't be giving my beer away; I cannot support anyone else's habit when I have my own. We need to get something straight. Just because you go to church, don't come here trying to change me. I am not ready for that now. Did you give my cigarettes away too?"

He sipped his Dr. Pepper. That made me even madder. What was he thinking that encouraged him to give my stuff away? I nagged for a while and realized it was no use.

When I cooled down, he said he had to leave. He kissed me on the forehead, and we walked outside.

The few beers he didn't give away, I drank and got tipsy. Reflecting on Mr. Mandingo: he was strange . . . not ordinary.

Time rocked on. One Saturday night, November 1998, we drove to Tyler, Texas, to see Willie Neal Johnson and the Canton Spirituals in concert. As usual, we enjoyed each other's company, singing, and having a good time. Santavia, in the backseat, quiet as a mouse, played with her doll. Out of nowhere, he asked, "Will you be my wife?"

I was numb. I looked at him, blushing, and with a bright smile, said, "Drive this car David Jr!" He gave me his genuine Jack's cookie smile and kept rolling. I didn't feel worthy of being his wife, and what happened to the one knee and the ring? He wasn't the romantic type like I'd been used to in the past, but he was tangible. He bribed me with his generosity, unlike the pretty boys I dated, loving the mirror more than I did, or the Romeos with the gifts, the drinks, the weed, the money, you name it. I got it all from those guys except one thing: this man wanted *me* to be his *wife*! I never in my life thought about a husband. Maybe except for a game in junior high. I looked over at him. He sang and drove; I hummed and thought.

Although my grandmother and grandfather were married, the older women taught me you had something good if you dated a good man. Plus, he had no children, so I didn't have to deal with baby mama drama. I'd hit the jackpot but couldn't accept it. He was ready for marriage; I wasn't. I had just accomplished a great thing in my life; I built a small house in Moscow, Texas, in my early twenties. Becoming a wife—I was not listening to that. I'd been on the street for almost nine years, making things happen on my own, now this? Marriage?

I needed to think about this one for a while. The thoughts ran through my mind. I didn't say yes or no to David that night. As usual, we had a good time at the concert. And I tried not to think about it.

Approximately one month after the concert, I acted like the chic that died and came back to life. I picked a fight trying to run David off; that didn't work. I worried. I didn't know how to be a wife. I observed how to cook and clean but realized there was more to it.

One day, he came to the house, and I yapped, yapped, yapped. He looked at me, puzzled, "What's wrong with you?"

"I don't know what's wrong with me. I'm a woman! I don't want to tie the knot, David Jr. You're a great guy, but you're too good for me."

"If that's the way you want it. But I will never shack with you."

You could hear a pin drop. In my mind, what's wrong with shacking? I didn't say a mumbling word. That street woman lived in me still, but David Jr. was different. During our months of dating, not one time did he stay all night. He drove from Coldspring and vice versa to visit, but he didn't sleep over.

After our little spat, he wasn't aware, but I slowed down smoking cigarettes and drinking Budweiser and Schlitz Malt Liquor Bull beers, and completely stopped the marijuana.

A couple of weeks later, one Saturday evening, he came to visit. I was furious and tipsy.

"The Lord sees us fornicating, David Jr.! You won't stay all night, and you certainly respect your parents. What about God? And don't expect me to go to church every Saturday night! I am young, and I'm still going out with my friends some Saturday nights!"

I never heard him use this tone before. "Is that what you think? I love you; I do what I do to keep you happy! I can wait to be intimate; you are the one with that problem! I'm not stopping you! Go out with your friends. You don't have to go to church, but I'm going."

I was speechless. His actions persuaded me the man was serious.

Nevertheless, time rocked on. One evening a genuine guy buddy stopped by my house. Back then, I had a man for everything . . . to wash my car, cut the grass, change a flat tire. This fellow was my handyman. We were outside, standing by my car talking. Low and behold, guess who drove up? Oh, brother, we had our misunderstanding a few days ago, and now this. DG got out of his car, making the other fellow look two feet tall.

"Evening," the guy said to David, Jr.

"Evening," David replied with an ugly look on his face. Of course, I introduced them, and I thought that was that.

My helper didn't leave. He stood there as if we were in a relationship. Oh, Lord, help me. Is he okay? Is he special? All these thoughts were running through my head about my handyman. At the time, I assumed we were cool, you know, just genuine friends. Well, he showed me a different side of him that day. Handy had some nerves, and Goffney was pissed. Is this my fault? I wondered. Heck naw, I'm not the one with the poor understanding. Since I had some say so, the conversation was over. We left my handyman standing outside alone and walked into the house.

David's look on his face was like, "Are you hiding something from me?"

"Heck naw! I do not do short men, for one. I like them, tall, tall, and tall. When I put my heels on, he still needs to be taller than I am." Unfortunately, it wasn't a laughing matter. "And for the record, there hasn't been any competition for Mr. Goffney." End of discussion, I convinced him the old boy had no place in my heart. The dust settled.

After about three weeks, I had time to reflect. I rejected calls from male friends, crying, wishing it weren't so. How could this be? I was dating a real man and I didn't want him? I missed our laughs, our dinner dates, and his kindness. Before I realized it, we were on the phone chit-chatting. What colors would the groomsmen wear?

CHAPTER 6
Family

Unlike many brides with twelve months to prepare for a wedding, I had six. Picking the colors was easy, considering our favorite color was royal blue. We added silver and white to enhance the ceremony. Trying to work and plan a wedding was challenging. I was frustrated and all over the place. Nevertheless, Saturday, June 26, 1999, in Coldspring, Texas, at God's Restoration Revival Center Holiness Church, under the leadership of Bishop David Lee Goffney Sr., I married my boyfriend, my man, and my mandingo.

For a couple of months, I complained about what went wrong at my wedding. David Jr. tried his best to appease me, "Sweetie, everything was fine. Let it go."

"You don't get it, do you? It wasn't fine; you were in such a hurry to start our honeymoon, I didn't get a chance to dance in my fancy wedding dress. Do you know how much we paid for that dress? We should have gone to the courthouse to get hitched if my big day was going to turn out the way it did."

He did what he usually does: let me vent. Over time, I finally let it rest. And our marriage journeyed on from there.

Being newlyweds excited us. Many predicted the world would end in the year 2000. Where that came from, I had no idea. I had a little fun preparing him a keepsake he would have forever. This souvenir allowed him to have me in his life regardless of the year. A lady posted a flyer describing her business as a photographer for marriages in our local grocery store. Her flyer persuaded me to have my husband a millennium calendar made in December 1999, just in time for the holidays.

Christmas morning, he opened his big box wrapped in gold and tied with a beautiful red bow. I watched and thought to myself, "It's the small things that need large packages." He was shocked to see such a huge box holding a calendar and a photo album. His eyes bucked, and his smile stretched as he turned the page. He oohed and awed for each calendar month. One of his favorites, the June bride: the veil was thrown to the back, and the rest of the sleek garment was white. Yes, please . . .

So, this was what marriage was? Not so bad. I could do this. We were no longer fornicating, and we saw one another daily. We were great together: going on family outings, making decent money, going to church, paying our tithes, saving a few dollars. We enjoyed every bit.

Besides the good life, in the fall of 2000, we were pregnant with our second baby, a loving family. This relationship was how it was supposed to be. Okay, I could do this. Marriage was not so bad. Things were going so well that David Jr. became Honey. Our path was straight and peaceful.

One day, in 2000, a family member introduced us to the "Hot Shot Business." The business included an F550 pickup truck, a forty-eight-foot gooseneck trailer, tarps, insurance for the driver, and the loads. After discussing the need to begin the process, I had a bad feeling about this business. I don't like losing money I don't have to lose. In the past, I've made a

$100 investment; it's easier to get over that. This decision was more than a $100 venture. With little education about running a business like this, we did it anyway.

Why did we do that? We just got married a few months ago. Not even a year. Oh HECK! Not wanting to admit we both made the decision, we began petty bickering, "If you had prayed more consistently, this mess wouldn't have happened!" That was me. Every curse word that came to mind, I blabbed out. Not only did I have some heartache in the streets; however, I didn't want to go through that being a married woman, especially if I could do bad by myself.

The truth was, I wasn't firm enough to say we shouldn't start a business needing more money to begin with. Five figures were a lot of money for kids of our status. That's what we learned we needed after the fact. We didn't have a clue what we were doing. Listening to the world around us, yes, it sounded like a great idea, maybe, but not at the time. Unfortunately, the decision drained our savings account. After this heartache and pain, we talked about, "Oh, if only we would have borrowed against our money and only if we would have done this or that." But "if only" was too late.

We gave the business a certain amount of time. If things didn't progress, we agreed not to stress. We'd surrender and let the doggone thing go.

Well, it didn't take long to see how the situation played out. One driver took the truck to Dallas and abandoned it, causing us time and money to pick the truck up. That was enough for me. I needed no more writing on the wall to let go.

Although the Hot Shot Business tortured me often, expecting our second unborn daughter helped me forget about what happened. I tidied up my tiny house, happy she would arrive soon. As the days passed in late August, my crazy father-in-law called being silly, "Shelett, September is right around the corner. Don't have that baby before my birthday."

"Aww, Bishop. I won't. I told you already her due date is September 17, my mom's birthday."

"I tell you what, Shelett Goffney, if that baby isn't born September 12, you can't eat another meal at my house!"

My father-in-law loved being silly. My sweet mother-in-law in the background, yelled, "David! Leave that pregnant woman alone. She's not in the mood for your mess."

"Let him tease, Mother-in-Law. If he didn't joke, I'd think something was wrong with him." We continued our smart talk, having a good time, not knowing what the month of September held.

Early one morning family called and asked if I had seen the news.

When I turned on the television, sure enough, every channel informed of the terrorist attacks. Terrorist attacks!? It was September 11, 2001. Around eight that morning, the destruction involved four planes. Several human beings were trained to commit suicide and kill others. A few hijackers operated two planes that attacked the Twin Towers in New York City; the news soon reported a third plane hit the Pentagon near Washington, DC, and the fourth plane crashed in Pennsylvania. What I didn't grasp, but discovered later, was that the passengers on the fourth plane got wind of what happened to the Twin Towers in New York City and the Pentagon in Washington, DC. The reporters announced that many hostages on the fourth plane called home to say their goodbyes. But before their lives ended, several fought a good fight.

The buildings were on fire, and all I witnessed was

immense black smoke clouds. I cried and cried, all day. Was the commotion real? Was this happening? It felt like the US stopped and started back in slow motion.

The next day misery crept in, and I was not sure if I was in labor or heartbroken from 9/11. My husband gathered my bag, and we headed to the hospital. Once we arrived on the second floor, the nurses prepped me to deliver our baby girl—one of the happiest/saddest days for me. I brought a life into the world, while approximately twenty-four hours prior, terrorists took lives out. After that tragedy, the planet was different. New laws and offices came into effect—one, to be exact, was Homeland Security. In a nutshell, what that meant was that at the airports, people get to experience a TDC moment without being criminals. When you go through the airport now, you have to walk through a metal detector, get patted down, and have your bags checked thoroughly. Many of us prayed for the families affected by 9/11, trusted God, and gently carried on.

As time slowly healed the country, we moved from Corrigan, Texas, to Coldspring, Texas. I took care of my responsibilities: cooking, cleaning, and loving my husband and our two daughters. So far, it was a cakewalk. The music sounded in the air, family and friends were well, and we had a balanced life.

Then, all of a sudden, I got distracted by David's career. He came from work one evening and told me his company was limiting the work hours. Why did they do that? Goodness! I despised hourly wage jobs; give me salary pay. At least this way, I would have a sound understanding of my paychecks. My husband didn't worry about a thing.

I never liked having low funds or low anything, to tell the truth. We had been married for two years. Transitioning from a single woman to a married woman with children was challenging for me. The battle of "woman vs. woman" became real. Taking care of one or two people, I had mastered, but now there were four of us. My husband, myself, Santavia, and Sanshae, the newborn, living on the same wage or less.

I was twenty-nine years old. What the heck was I doing? One day I ran into a young lady I socialized with, and she told me how she enrolled in the Texas School of Business. I got excited! I loved education, so this information was right up my alley. We had gotten out of the trucking industry, and I needed to sharpen my self-employed skills. I was like, "Oh God, this would be huge for our family. If you make a way, I'd love to attend the journey." A couple of months later, after completing the paperwork, I began the Texas School of Business and enjoyed every bit. The classes were structured to teach us to assist in the administrative department not to run our own corporation, so the training would be perfect to use later in any career.

As the days passed while I strived for my certificate, I received the Most Professional Award. And I no longer smoked cigarettes. My husband suggested I should do something nice for myself for the immense achievement. "I should do something for myself, if not for the achievement, at least for no longer smoking." So, I did. I went shopping. Whoo-hoo! I purchased a new outfit and a new pair of shoes for graduation. My eyes wanted to buy more, but I controlled my emotions, envisioning I'd have a job soon.

I graduated in November 2002 and began an intern with a company located off Interstate 45 south and 1960. Approximately ninety days later, the owner hired me full time. However, I took for granted the women helping me were okay with babysitting. We had only two girls. Santavia was in school during the day, and Sanshae was with either Grandma or Auntie.

Our focus at the time was to save for a car. Considering my husband and I didn't want many bills, we desired to pay cash.

One evening I picked Sanshae up from Auntie's house. But before I left, she wanted to have a heart-to-heart talk.

"Shelett, don't feel like you have to work so much. You and your husband are a great couple together. Y'all can survive even if you choose to stay home, especially if you both are planning to have more children."

"Aww, Auntie, thank you for the encouragement, but I don't think we're going to have any more babies."

Driving home after that hour chit-chat, I had a talk with the Lord. "I heard what she said, Lord, but I can't imagine your desire for us is to be broke and struggling; also, there is no doubt in my mind you want us to be able to help those in need, so that's why I accepted the position. Although the right thing to do is be home with my daughters, they also want things.

Santavia wishes to participate in cheerleading, sports, and whatever you can think of. She talked about staying busy most of the time, and don't let me forget to mention I found the career of my life. I've never made this much money. We can come up! Therefore, you do not want us without. Isn't that right, God?"

He didn't answer.

Never giving another thought to my aunt and mother-in-law being tired of babysitting, or just not wanting to spend their retirement caring for my daughters, I took it upon myself to believe they didn't mind. Distracted by my wants? Who, me? Naw . . . not me. In my defense, I had to help my family. So being the woman I was, I continued working.

The next morning, I woke up and did my routine. I went to the ladies' room, washed my hands, and gave God about three minutes of prayer. Honestly, probably two. I got G'd up—cute and sharp as a tack for work. I kept at least three pairs of black pants in my closet and several cute tops to limit my thought process of getting ready for the week. I gathered the girls' clothes together over the weekend or the night before. I packed our lunches faithfully, so when lunch break rolled around, my girlfriend and I were able to go shopping.

When I got to work, my coworkers had a strange look on their faces. I asked no questions, but I discerned they were troubled. I acted, as usual, happy and energetic. Besides, I had a job to do as an administrative assistant: smile for anyone who came through the door. With that said, I continued as if I wasn't bothered one bit; I turned my computer on, set my purse down, and put my lunch in the refrigerator.

An hour of the morning passed, and once the boss arrived and settled into his office, I heard him call my first name, "Roberta."

"Yes, sir?"

"Come have a seat." He explained that the company might not be in business much longer and I might not have a job. Tears formed, but they didn't fall . . . how terrible for him and for me.

"But I thought I found the career of my life," I said, raising my eyebrow as he continued.

Nonetheless, the moment broke my heart. I really did like that job. Unfortunately, the business ended; looked like I was jobless—so bittersweet. I prayed for the company. I would miss my coworker who found pleasure purchasing a $7 blouse to match our black pants instead of buying a $7 lunch. My motto: "The blouse lasts longer." On the flip side, I was happy to be home with my husband and girls.

Happier than a kid in the candy store, David sang a song of joy. He didn't verbally sing it, but his body language did and his tone of voice. "You do a fine job taking care of the girls and me. We will be okay." Easy for him to say. As long as I managed our spreadsheet, we were okay. I tried balancing my household like a good little wife, but some days the challenge defeated me.

One day a guy approached me about a vacuum business. Oh, wee. In this business, if I sold one item, I'd make big bucks. "Okay." My eyes gleamed. "Tell me more?" The opportunity sounded promising, and I informed my husband about it. "You do a wonderful job taking care of us. Why don't you consider taking care of us?" I guess the look on my face encouraged his mouth to utter, "But if you want to, I am here. I will support you in whatever you want to do," and he did. I took off like a racecar and pursued the business. The position consisted of late nights, and I wasn't aware of this initially. In sales, we had to finish the entire presentation and then let the customers critique the product. Oh brother, what was I thinking? My husband had to work late one particular day, and I picked the babies up late from auntie's.

My auntie socked it to me when I arrived at her house. "Shelett, you can NOT be working late at night, and you have a husband and two small girls at home."

"Oh Lord, please make her stop," I silently spoke in my head. She went on and on. I took the butt chewing like a big girl since she was telling the truth. That was the end of that profession. I had nothing to say to anybody, not even God. She ripped me a new one. When I got home, I had little to say. I put the girls to bed and went to bed myself. That butt chewing made me think . . . "Is this what they mean when they say the truth will set you free? Because I was free from that business?"

Time settled. I handled my wifely duties and took care of the home for about a year, and then I was back at hustling. I didn't want to, but I couldn't relax in the state we were in. Every time I worked on my spreadsheets and didn't reap the results I liked, I honestly thought I was doing the right thing for my family by running to the workplace or starting a business. My intentions were to substitute teach a couple of days a week at the school district, allowing me the opportunity to balance the rest of my days.

So far, so good, my plan seemed to be working. I labored as a sub for a few months, until one day, the principal stopped me in the hall. "Roberta, there's a full-time position as a paraprofessional. I would be honored if you were on our team full time." How could I say no to that? I didn't talk to God, my husband, nobody. I took the position. I didn't go there to stay. But at the time, my decision would benefit in two ways: a great asset to the district and my household. A win-win situation.

Also, I couldn't stay long. The state wasn't paying a lot of money, and some teachers had our relationship twisted. I was on campus to assist the teachers, students, and district, not to be bossed by teachers. I was the professor for the semester. We needed to delete and repeat. And we did. We started over with understanding, which brought love, peace, and happiness to our team.

Time voyaged on, and I often hated budgeting a spreadsheet, along with trying to be a good mama and wife. Managing, in addition to my other duties, was more than a notion. Getting another job, in my mind, was the answer. Who wants to be without and not enjoy the finer things in life? I didn't. And that's one reason I had a "get rich quick" attitude. The job guaranteed the money, allowing us to profit quicker.

Ha, ha, ha. That's what I thought until my husband came home one day and told me his hours scaled back on the job. "AGAIN!" Now our income became a wash, better known as an even exchange. What he didn't make, I made, no extra. Really, Lord? I guess I should have prayed about our situation instead of doing it my way. I called this my Pharaoh moment. Old Pharaoh initiated his own troubles by hardening his heart at times and doing things his way.

"God, was I wrong for wanting to help my family?" He didn't answer; therefore, I made the best of work. Time went on, and I enjoyed the school district. I met fantastic staff, teachers, students, and parents. Children are so easy to love, and many of them respected me to the fullest. One of my favorite times of the year was career day. I encouraged the students to be specific about what they wanted in life, and they would be fine. There were other occasions when I talked to women about marriage, children, church, finances, and more, and in return, they sowed into me. The mystery was worth it; I felt free and able to give myself away.

Days passed like a rollercoaster. I could not figure it out for the life of me what happened. How was it we were fine one minute and in trouble the next? I continued taking care of my responsibilities. After hours of sitting at the kitchen table figuring in my seventy-sheet spiral notebook, I had enough.

Tit for tat, not holding back, mad about everything, I wanted to move to Conroe, Texas.

"Honey, if we move, the grocery stores and pediatricians would be convenient."

David Jr. glanced into space.

"We could save immensely on gas, Honey."

He looked at the floor. He tried to convince me why we shouldn't move. In my mind, I questioned: "Is this why my parents separated? Is this why so many people get divorced? No understanding?" As soon as I decided to leave our marriage, guess what? We were pregnant with our third baby in 2004. God has a strange way of doing things, doesn't he?

Dang! I couldn't go anywhere. I had two babies and now one on the way; imagine dragging them up and down the road looking for a place to live when I already had a roof over my head—negative. Honey wasn't abusing me. If anything, I probably talked too much. Nevertheless, I found joy in my third pregnancy.

I couldn't take the challenge. The pressure wasn't my usual. I wanted his input on some decisions I made, but the way I approached him caused him to ignore me. It made me hotter than fish grease when I felt invisible. What was a girl to do? We were kids growing up together. Although my life seemed to be a mystery, I eventually calmed down. And with joy, I made the best of it.

I enrolled in Lone Star College and took a couple of online classes. Lord have mercy. I didn't have a clue what I was getting myself into taking online classes with small children and having to read boring history books. I got through it, but I knew with two little ones at home and another on the way, online courses were a no-no for me.

That summer in July, we had a get-together at the lake. I wanted peach cobbler so bad. Once I ate it, I got sick as a dog. I gagged all evening long. Peach cobbler never made me miserable like that. Honey took me home and tucked me into bed. Goodness. This kiddo must be David Jr. the third. Soon, time would tell.

Guess what? Yep, we had a girl on December 6, 2005, at 4:45 a.m. We named her Shani'ya. We came home and settled in with our new bundle of joy.

As the months passed, I felt like I could handle it, but just an orbit later, frustration boiled on the inside of me! Divorce stared me in the face. Santavia, sweet as could be, asked her dad one day, "Daddy, what's wrong with Mama?"

"I'm not sure, Ta, leave her alone."

"David Jr, I will not be pregnant and barefoot," I told him, raging with animosity, wishing and praying he'd say, "Okay, then let's get a divorce if you want." Nope, he didn't say a mumbling word. After all that raising cane, guess what? You got it. I was pregnant again with our fourth baby in 2006.

Surprise! Surprise? I could not believe I was expecting again! "Dang, did I miss a pill? I was too doggone submissive. Oh Lord, how will I face my sisters-in-laws, family members, and friends?" They would always say every time David and I went out of town, we would come back pregnant. I guess there is power in the tongue. Ha-ha-ha. We laughed together and got through it one last time.

As time progressed, my husband and I could not be intimate in my last trimester. It could have caused placental abruption. Our doctor thought it would be safer to remain abstinent until the baby was born. Talk about learning new ways of compassion.

September 5, 2007, around 2:00 a.m., I jumped out of bed soaking wet. "Honey! Wake up! WE GOTTA GO!"

"What? Are you sure, Bert? She's three weeks early!"

He grabbed my bags, and we headed to the hospital. Oh my, what a ride. Once we got there, the nurses prepped me, and we prepared for delivery. Unfortunately, Shantel was breached; the doctor had to do a cesarean. He asked, "While I'm here, would you like to get your tubes tied?"

The words could not come out of my mouth fast enough. "Yes! Please!" Bringing our precious baby girl home began our journey as the Goffney Jr. Bunch.

By baby number four, I had figured it out. Honey never liked doing the "girly-girl" duties. He was horrible at it. He tried, bless his heart. If I told the truth, we both sucked at parenting small children. He gave her a bottle if that's all he had to do. As soon as something challenging happened, like changing a dirty diaper or calming her down, I could hear my name echoing in the atmosphere. "Sweetie, sweetie, I cannot calm her down." Lord help, I couldn't take a simple shower. What I did know was, Mr. Goffney knew how to call for "Sweetie."

CHAPTER 7
Trouble in My Way

As life journeyed on, David insisted I stay home to keep the children, which would benefit the whole family. He pointed out my strengths as a wife and mother. Yes, I budgeted, bartered, couponed, and babysat for others to make ends meet, but when I worked, went to college, and had additional responsibilities, Honey noticed we didn't get along well. Although I understood what he said, I battled with the woman who chased a life she had with a big imagination, before a husband and children, not realizing I was no longer my own.

Our oldest daughter, Santavia, reminded me how much she appreciated everything I did to make her dreams come true. I knew she loved me. She always tried to help with her sisters.

"Mom, I can help you change Pooda's diaper."

"Pooda? Who is Pooda?"

"Shantel, Mama."

"Oh, okay."

"Thank you, baby; Mama really appreciates that."

She was such a good kid. That day she gave her baby sister a nickname.

Any sport she wanted to participate in, I made it happen. Why? I was the little girl on Snow Hill Road who wished, so desperately, to be a cheerleader. And for Santavia *not* to be a cheerleader wasn't an option for me; striving to make it happen for my baby girl and doing without myself was my only answer. If push came to shove, I would have sold a glass of lemonade. People love to support when a person has a great cause.

Like any other typical night, everyone was in bed, and I talked with the Lord about our situation.

"I did not go to work at the school district when I did to get rich quick, Lord. It was for the things the money took care of: the mortgage note, light bill, water bill, diapers, giving to others, a balanced life.

Need I say more? Our children were twelve, almost thirteen; five, nearly six; one, almost two; and now a newborn. I needed an overflow. The understanding of the ordinary things money took care of drove me. Was I wrong, Lord?"

He didn't answer.

Life rocked on. I went back to work when Shantel turned three months old in December 2007. I enjoyed my babies immensely, but I missed the company of my coworkers. Once I got back to work, I didn't think the pressure of missing my babies would be so intense. My emotions were all over the place. I had a feeling I wanted to work. Then I had the feeling I wanted to be home.

I never had a "kick your heels up" moment. My duties at work were pleasurable, but reflecting on my responsibilities, for example, picking the two older girls up from practice and the smaller two up from the babysitter was a thorn in my flesh. Around this time, Santavia was thirteen, Sanshae was six, Shani'ya was two, and Shantel was a newborn. I thought I could do both, work and pay the babysitters (my mom and mother-in-law) and take care of the home.

But was that the right thing for me at the time?

Back then . . . I couldn't even answer that question.

My liveliness rose when I could help my family at home and others on the outside; there was something about it. My husband couldn't understand this, and eventually, I had to face reality: I could not be in two places at one time. I didn't want to leave the loving staff I met, but the need to be home overpowered the need for work. I took a deep breath, exhaled, and continued with life.

I walked through the house one day, while the family was chilling watching TV, with a broom in my hand and the other on my hip.

"There are two kinds of people in the world: people that watch things happen, and people that make things happen."

I had no idea where that came from. Observation? I liked TV sometimes, but if my husband and I were going to retire one day and be productive, we could not do it "watching," we had to "do."

Having a champagne taste on a beer budget wasn't easy to get rid of. Although I didn't drink, during this time, my wants hadn't changed.

My family couldn't see what I saw. Or is it I could not see what they could see? The umph it took to manage a house of six wasn't much, but consistency was the key, and I knew this. Honey encouraged me, "You're doing a *great* job taking care of us." He got one thing right: it was a job! I didn't like to work and watch them enjoy the fruits of my labor. In my eyes, we were a team. As a woman, sometimes, I felt like I did it *all*! Working, cooking, cleaning, going to college online or in person, taking the kid(s) to basketball practice, taking care of other children, sometimes hustling on the side, balancing the spreadsheet, and the list went on and on. By this year, I wanted no encouragement. I knew how to encourage myself. I needed some *help*.

One day our conversation was so heated, I thought we were going to fight! For real.

"God doesn't want us in this predicament, Honey!"

"Is it God, or is it you?"

"What do you mean, Honey?"

"I try to keep you happy, sweetie! Just forget it," and he stormed out of the house.

I thought to myself, "Now you want to wait until I have all these babies to act like that— just like a man. I didn't mean to push him, but he needed to see it my way, or was it I needed to see it his? We've always had what we needed, but what was it? I was crazy about him one minute and wanting to beat him up the next.

After fuming and threatening to sleep in our baby daughter's room, I heard my girlfriend's voice saying, "You two have a beautiful marriage. Don't let the enemy have you sleeping in the other room." I snatched my pillow, huffed and puffed down the hall, and went to bed. Tell me why that's the best hanky-panky ever. I wondered if that was one reason we went tit for tat—to make up. We both apologized for our behavior, and the dust settled. I convinced him that I should get another job, and we moved on from there.

In 2008, I left the school district as a paraprofessional and went back to TDCJ. I met an amazing lady who became my baby's caregiver through the same lady I attended Texas School of Business with. By this time, our baby girl had turned a year old. Oh, the caregiver was one of the missing pieces in my life. "Lady, where have you been all my life! You are a perfect fit." My husband didn't understand. Yes, I could have done it; however, it was not an easy assignment being the woman in my shoes. She loved to braid my girl's hair, and every Friday, they were football ready! Thank you, Lord. I had a flashback about some days when I had to wash and condition their hair. I did well enough to get by. No, I wouldn't say I liked combing hair. Nor did I love my hair straightened. As a little girl, getting my hair combed was not my fun day. Ouch! Take it easy on my nappy hair. I asked Honey once to help me with the girls' hair, and bless his heart, he couldn't take the rubber band off the ponytail.

I needed some help from a woman who knew what she was doing. She used her natural talent(s) babysitting and braiding hair. Thank you, Lord.

I worked in the same unit I did in 1997, before I met my husband. What? Thompson, is that you? Some remembered me by my maiden name, not remembering my married name. It was a work reunion, so good to see everybody and vice versa.

I journeyed on to work. I dared not share the issues at the unit with my husband, considering he didn't want me there anyway, especially if I had to suit up. He was already unhappy with the fact that I went back. We talked about it, and I told him, let's give it a chance and see what happens. Let's go with the flow.

If I was wrong, I would come back home and finish college. I wanted to do that anyway. However, I could not focus on college, knowing we had girls who loved to participate in activities and we liked to give to others and try to build our wealth. On top of that, the world was going through a recession in 2008.

I finally got him to soften up a little, and life went on. Everything I said I would do, I did the opposite. I didn't realize it at first, but dust formed on my spreadsheet. Shoot, I didn't need to budget; I had my whole paycheck. Can you say cha-ching? There's nothing like having what you desire. But it wasn't long before I realized this couldn't be the way forever.

One day we were in the control picket, and four of us were chit-chatting. A heated dispute broke out, and I said, "Ain't nobody perfect." I could feel my spirit tug on me. Total quietness settled in the room. That day, I knew I was wrong. How could the phrase, "Practice makes perfect," not make sense? What came over me? Why did I say that when I believed what my grandmother taught me? Granny instilled in me, the more you do anything, the better you are at it. Later that evening, as I drove home, I asked the Lord to forgive me. I knew I was wrong, but I couldn't prove why. Time moved on, and I knew I was forgiven, and I didn't think about it anymore.

One night, after I had been back at TDCJ for about a year, there was an escape at our unit. When an escape occurred at the prison, correctional officers had to post near the highway or wherever the officer stationed them. Oh Lord, my husband would have a fit if they put me on the side of the road. It wouldn't be long, and he would suggest that I give my job my two weeks' notice. Gratefully, I never had to post on the outside of the unit.

Back at home, safe and sound, everyone was sleeping, or at least I thought everyone was sleeping. And suddenly, we heard a big boom! I jumped up and ran down the hall, and there stood Ta and CC crying! I was screaming, "What's wrong!" I looked in the restroom, and Shani'ya had cut off all of Shantel's hair. Y'all, I lost it!

Santavia (Ta) said, "Momma, don't spank her. She didn't know!"

Shani'ya had a look on her face that said, "What? It's only hair, why y'all trippin'?" We all cried. Poor Shani'ya, everybody was shaking their heads. Shani'ya had a severe look on her face. "It's just hair."

I realized then I had too many children to be working such long hours. We lived with it. We looked at the situation like Shani'ya did—it was hair. It would grow back. And we kept it moving.

The weekend rolled around. It was our tenth wedding anniversary. I knew we would have a good time. Occasions liked this were worth the drama. We went to Corpus Christi, Texas, and I had one of the best times of my life. At this time, we had a fourteen-year-old, an eight-year-old, a three-year-old, and a twelve-month-old at home, and we were so thankful to be getting a break.

I didn't get a chance to swirl much, oh, but when we went out of town, that was my chance to "dance." What a life, enjoying it with my boyfriend, my man, and my husband. And the dance floor, baby! Yeah! Does anybody want to dance? Come on, Mr. Goffney; let's dance . . . Let's boogie! Heyyyyy!

Soon after our tenth anniversary, I left TDCJ. I knew I couldn't go there to stay. I didn't murmur about it; I was sick of getting up at 2:40–3:00 a.m., packing lunches and backpacks, getting the girls' clothes together, and making a list for the fifteen-year-old to help her morning go smoother when she woke her little sister Sanshae. Plus, I dropped the two smaller children off at the babysitter at 4:00 a.m. Yeah, after a year and a half of that, I let it go with a two weeks' notice.

That summer, 2010, the Goffney family went on vacation to Las Vegas. Yes. My messy father-in-law was the head honcho. Gosh, we love him. It was eleven of us total, a family road trip. Whoo-hoo! I loved a good time. All the kids rode in the truck with us. I know it drove my husband crazy. Rolling his eyes in the back of his head, he reminded us on several occasions we were too loud. We smiled at one another, and it was my perfect chance to ask, "You want to have a truck full of babies?" He dropped his chin and looked at me like I was crazy. I couldn't help but laugh. We made unforgettable memories that summer. I recall my husband buying a suitcase, and everyone called it a baby casket. Ha, ha, ha, anyone ashamed? Yes, yes, and yes . . .

That was one of the best vacations of our life. We made unforgettable memories.

I felt so good around this time. Everything was going well. You know, the way life is supposed to be. I traveled to the nursing home(s) to visit loved ones and their roommates. I loved the little ladies. I felt free when I did good works; I knew they appreciated me sharing time with them. Something as simple as brushing their hair or polishing their nails was a pleasure.

Midafternoon, one of the head chiefs called and instructed me to come over to pick up my bag of name brand items. She understood how I loved to ball on a budget. When she found a sale, she looked out for me. And in return, I took her cash to pick up my items.

On this day, I guess I hesitated too long. She asked, "Are you coming? And don't forget your $20." There was a pause. "Gal, do you hear me?" she asked with a louder voice. "I know you have $20—a girl of your status. Now come on here. I don't have all day." I grabbed my car keys and ran out the door, shucking. The older woman didn't care what she said—and she meant it. Guess what? I got my tail over there with *$25*. You got that right: I took a tip; I learned to make $20 do tricks.

Time journeyed on, I had my new threads, I was the CEO making my schedule. When the girls were in school, I picked up their slack, and I cut myself a check. I earned this position. Lol. It's real.

Homemakers come with a price tag. And don't let me get started on my stockpile. Shucks, I prepared meals that fed six people, and goodness, I wouldn't say I liked to cook. But I loved taking care of my family.

Besides my spreadsheet and couponing, I pursued my hustle in other areas. To name one: I met a wonderful lady, joined a business, and became a beauty consultant. This business didn't keep me out late at night; I could do this. Not only did I enjoy the company, but I enjoyed the products. I took pleasure in helping other women take care of their skin and selecting their products. I journeyed nine years as a beauty consultant.

For several reasons I needed to own my own business, primarily the tax breaks. I had a lot of distractions in my life; however, this one I got right.

This season came with many perks. I dropped the girls off at school and traveled to a clients' house to present my products. I not only helped my customers, but I returned home before school was out and cooked dinner. I had my cake and ate it too. What a life. I got a glimpse of what it should have been.

CHAPTER 8

Babysitter

Just when I thought I could live in the moment forever, one summer I had my children and many other kids at my house. Some days were beautiful, no worries. All the kids got along, and I managed. Then one day, something happened, and I thought of pulling my hair—or somebody's hair—out. The kiddoes whipped my behind. I told all the chill-ren and their parents: "Go Home! I'm not keeping any more brats for a while." I was so tired, I couldn't even say "children."

Wait. Let me back up and tell you what happened. One day I had to take a timed test on the computer. The babies were supposed to be sleeping, considering it was nap time. Low and behold, while in the office, I heard an unfamiliar noise in the other room. I ran out, and on the kitchen floor sat a flour-faced kid—what a mess. With my hands on my hips, I stood in awe. The little rascal looked at me, grinning. Was I big mad, little mad, tickled, or sad? And the kiddo wasn't my biological baby. "You little mischievous thing, you were supposed to be taking a nap." There went my grade.

After a few days, I got over my sensitivity, especially when one kid called and asked if they could come over. I was such a flunky. But that's what my love did, denied itself.

When it came to my babies, I couldn't tame my emotions. But some days, they were off the chain! The rug rats whipped my tail. After that summer, I got a job to buy a break. Can I be real? I love the children, not the "job" of babysitting.

Babysitters are one of the *best* groups of people in the world. It takes special folks to babysit daily. Without sitters or daycare, many of us could not have accomplished some of the things our hearts desired.

For us who have been helpers one to another, thank you immensely. As your babysitter, I appreciate you understanding me to the core. I'm so grateful to have you all in my life. My firm ways didn't keep you from loving me. We stayed logical and not emotional. And that's what kept us together.

To my babysitters, my hat's off to you; I've learned from experience, it is not an easy task babysitting, nor is the responsibility mandatory for you. I can never pay you for what you're worth, but I will strive to help you succeed in what you wish for, no matter what. Why? You deserve it to infinity. You sat behind the scenes so I could accomplish some desires for me, my family, and others. Thank you immensely for what you have done. I pray I've proven I'll always be by your side.

There are three types of babysitters from my point of view. One type loves babysitting; taking care of children is their niche. They would rather babysit than do any other occupation. How do I know this? I asked and drilled my babysitters until they almost cursed me out, just kidding. But I needed clarity in answering if they desired looking after my children? No matter what their answer would have been, I would have respected it.

Then there's the second babysitter who tries it a time or two, and honestly, they will not "rock-a-bye baby." Their final answer is no. They don't worry about people's "feelings." They're logical and know that childcare is not for them.

Then, the third babysitter sometimes wants to babysit and other times does not. In their defense, several barely comprehend what they are doing themselves.

Once upon a time, that was me, the third babysitter. With my children and others, but someone had to do it. You see: some will, some will not, I might.

Let me pause a minute. This section's remainder wasn't written to sound like a sermon; however, you need to read. You might learn something.

Tip #1: We must remember some women would love to have a child/children but can't. Having babies just because is not a joke to me. The bundle of joy is a living, breathing being that we are accountable for. So, as you continue reading this section, remember: they transfer from hands to hands, but at the end of the day, who's responsible?

Tip #2: As a babysitter, I suggest the parent(s) be careful how they approach their sitter. For example, "I'm going to pay you. Can you watch the kids until I get back?" Well, I know you're going to pay me. See the difference? Would a person walk into the daycare and say, "I'm going to pay you?" Of course not, because as a parent, they realize that's a place of business. One must treat the babysitter like the daycare—a business. Imagine in your mind how you would walk into the daycare, speak to the one in charge, and receive information, etcetera. The daycare's services aren't free. Nor is a woman's side hustle. Some guardians have a set price of what they're planning to pay their sitter. That's not how business works, especially if your sitter is like me. I set the price, not the parent. Take it or leave it. Show appreciation to your sitter. Yes, laughing and talking is okay, but when it comes to your precious cargo, that's business, baby.

Tip #3: If the sitter upsets you, be the parent who says, "I'll make other arrangements." You still have to get someone to keep your precious responsibility. Stay logical; you can't grow if you don't know—that's the truth. Just because a person is home does not mean they're in the babysitting profession. However, handling a situation like its business is best. The homemaker, a.k.a. the real housewife, sometimes has plans of her own. You never know what door may open for her. Did you know Florida Evans (Esther

Rolle), who played the mom on *Good Times*, was about forty-four years old when she began her acting career? I asked this question to keep your mind clear of other's opportunities. Although the sitter is home all day, the root is deeper than the surface. One may assume the sitter is home doing nothing; however, she might be sharpening her skills, whether it's dancing, financial, writing, whatever. It's her time. Never assume. When one assumes, they make an ass/u/me.

Tip #4: If a person does not want me talking about God, Jesus, and the Holy Ghost, then keep your precious baby/babies' home with you. I'll never be ashamed of my God.

Tip #5: Communicate well with anyone who helps you along the way. When you take your babies to the daycare or babysitter, remind the ladies, with a pure heart, that without them, you couldn't be who you are. I understand why some people have nannies. The nannies can be right by the parents' side. She can set a price, and the parent can either accept or deny the offer. That's understanding.

On the other hand, when you cannot have a nanny,

it hurts sometimes putting yourself on the back burner, but that's one of the consequences of having a child or children. You may not be able to spread your wings far.

Tip #6: Don't feel obligated to babysit for everyone because you are home babysitting your own. You call the shots. I realize you love the babies. So, do I, but keeping it real, they're going to grow up. And one day the parents are not going to need you. If you decide to carry on, for example, on Friday and Saturday nights when the daycare is closed, take the payment, not gifts. Here's why: you need to use that money to invest, buy dividend stocks, or invest in whatever you can to receive a return on investment. Some parents thought I was crazy when I told them, "I appreciate the gifts, but give me the money to invest." You see, if I buy stocks, eventually the dividends will allow me to buy that same gift more than once. Don't get me wrong, I like gifts, but not as much as I like stock. Think about it. If you babysit for sixteen years and you invest part of your babysitting earnings, then your money will grow as your baby grows.

Tip #7: Please, listen and listen well. The best thing for any parent to do is to put your child/children in daycare, keep them yourself, or draw up a contract with your babysitters. I understand outlining an arrangement is uncomfortable, but it's best. Paperwork will cut down on a bunch of that he-said, she-said stuff.

Tip #8: Don't believe the hype when someone says you'll never be ready for a child. Stop and ask these questions? Are they saying that because no one taught them? Did my parent(s) or guardian teach me how to be ready for a family? Did anyone warn me that I may or may not be able to afford daycare or a nanny? Did I learn anything as a child from observation in my own home? What if my husband leaves me with two children and one on the way? Are funds put back that will assist during decision-making? Are you planning on going back to work? If so, who will babysit? Have my husband and I talked about one of us staying home if we must?

Yes, some folks will say God has the last say-so. That is the *truth*. On the contrary, God left me to teach you through my experience, so you don't make some of the same mistakes. My warnings may save you a lot of tears. What people will not tell you is that a moral babysitter is not always available. God blessed me to have virtuous caregivers. But you may have to stay home with your precious baby. Stay logical.

This chapter is about being educated when you have a family and what to do. It's some guidance.

When I worked out of town, my mother-in-law or auntie picked my babies up from practice. I knew they didn't mind; however, I dug deeper. As women get older and retire, they may or may not tell you they don't want to be your cab driver. Think about it. Suppose it's five o'clock in the evening, and another woman has to stop what she's doing to pick up your responsibility. I felt guilty. Although I paid my sitters, I put myself in their shoes. I asked myself the question, "Am I going to want to battle with children at the age of sixty?" Me being me, my answer was, "Heck naw!" Once I raise my four children, I've done my due diligence. Don't get me wrong. I love all my babies, I'll always be there for them, and if I had to do it all over again, I would in a heartbeat.

In larger cities, there may be an Uber driver for children after school. Perhaps someone trustworthy can start a business in a small town to help working parents by providing after-school programs.

Tip #9: It amazes me that we teach people how to be rich, but not many teach how to be parents. *Financial freedom*, I hear this everywhere. But who's teaching babysitter freedom? What does it profit the sitter to be financially free but have no "time" to be free? Ask questions before deciding to start a family. It's okay to wait. The truth is, some situations may be different from yours. For example, some parent(s) do not have to change their own child's/children's diaper; they do not have to raise a hand to parent. This situation may not be yours. You may have to be the mother and the father.

Raising a family was designed to be stress-free.

Tip #10: I wasn't used to being a mother without a paycheck. I made my own money and heard the voices of others. If you need more money, get a job. If you get a job, you can get ahead. Is this true? Not necessarily when the outcome is an even exchange. So if this is you and you love making that cha-ching, keep using your birth control. I want you to be able to witness your babies take their first step and say their first word. When their tummy aches, there is no one like Mama. I say this to you because I lived it. I was there for my babies regardless of how I went to the workplace; I was home more than not. It was crazy the way my days played out, but I did it. I kept battling with the woman who told me to stay home and the woman telling me I could do it, go to work, or start a business. Anything you want, you can still accomplish while raising your child/children. Getting ahead may take a little bit longer, but it's doable. In my head, the other woman told me, "Girl, you know you have to buy all four of your babies those tennis shoes. You don't favor one over the other." "Girl, you can't afford it if you don't go back to work. It's almost Christmas time." "What are you going to do? If you go into the stash, David will ask questions, and you don't want to hear that mess." After that thought, I went to work. Some of my decisions were to spoil the Goffney girls. I told them no at times, but the idea of my babies not having like I didn't have wasn't an option for me. Life caught me between a rock and a hard place. If I had to choose to be a noble mother, a great employee, or a committed business partner, I preferred my rocks: my family. Besides, I heard the voices of the older women, back in the day, who babysat. They would say, "Some parents forget where they come from." I never wanted that to be me.

Therefore, I decided to take care of my *own* children. I discovered why they said that though: the parent/parents do not return to get the babysitter. They leave them behind and follow folks they just met. Let me explain. I've had the opportunity to rub elbows with millionaires. Some millionaires said to me, "Roberta, to be successful and live your 'dreams' you have to let some people go." With my fingers folded together and circling my thumbs, I listened. But let me help the world. That "quote" is not clear. If I didn't understand, I would have walked off and left my family. First of all, I chose to do the hanky-panky, so my babies are my responsibility. It's no longer about my dreams. Understanding that is the first lesson to those who hear that quote. Secondly, I met you yesterday, millionaire. So, you're telling me to leave the folks who have had my back for years and listen to you because you're a millionaire? Negative. My common sense persuaded me if I devote my husband's paycheck to the bills and save and invest mine, we can still be millionaires. Lastly, I returned to encourage the babysitters. I introduced my sitters to others in high positions. Many sitters have a talent that hasn't been revealed. Maybe it's because she put herself on the backburner. Isn't it only right to come back for her? With that said, I share the wealth. Helping others recognize their talent(s) is sharing the wealth, not just giving money. Sharing the wealth is deeper than the surface. We all have opportunities. But the truth is, a few women get so wrapped up in childcare that they forget they have more to offer. I believe in bringing people with me, not leaving them behind. Now, once I have offered and have "truly" tried in ways more than monetary, then I wash my hands. That said, don't forget the people who helped you. They don't need your money; they need your assistance in helping them reveal their talent(s).

Tip #11: For the young ladies on your way to being mothers, you'll love your children immensely, but the truth is, you don't laugh and play all day every day. Some days draw tears out of you. I'm not telling you not to have a family. I would love for you to have at least four children. But I want you to enjoy each of them instead of sitting at the kitchen table late at night crying to God because you're drowned in bills or credit card debt, all because you bought a lot of stuff and suddenly one of the parents had to be home, usually the mother.

Don't forget the parties every Friday and Saturday

night. Someone must keep the baby. You can't go to the club or go shopping with a friend if there's no one to look after the baby. One of your friend's husbands or moms may look after their baby for them, but you may not have that privilege.

How about buying shoes, perfume, clothes? Do those things for yourself for about three years of your career. This period will give you time to meet people, learn to invest, stay out late as long as you want to, and spend your money and time the way you want. Do fun things with your friends, college buddies, business partners, etcetera.

I loved to witness young ladies buying the car, house, condo, or whatever they envisioned before starting a family or having a child or children. Their victory gave me chills. I felt like the high school cheerleader I didn't get the chance to be. I cheered them on! That's right, girlfriend. Do you. And don't be ashamed of being husbandless or babyless. Take your time.

Now, if you are young and have a child, it's okay. You can still soar. Anything you envision, you can bring to life. But I must keep it 100. Once you have a baby, you are no longer your own.

Tip #12: "It's Mama's baby; Papa's maybe." The baby's daddy may or may not be in the child/children's life. Much of the time, it is the mother who raises her baby or babies. For the first seven years of your adult life—usually ages eighteen to twenty-five—you're still finding yourself. Think about that, seven years. You may not see it yet, but that's not long at all. Here's a reminder: your parents have been bossing you for eighteen years, trying to teach you the way, and now you're going to start a family to boss you around? Believe it or not, that's what's going to happen.

I acted like the CEO, the Boss, the "all that," but I still had the phone ringing and people asking, "Where are you? We miss you." That right there drives you home. So, take a minute and reflect on who you are and who you'll be in your children's eyes. You are your baby's superstar. I'm not saying not to pursue your visions. Just don't chase your visions solely at others' expense without a sound understanding.

Tip #13: The time may come that a sitter has had a rough day. Don't ever tell the sweet child, "Don't ask to go back over there! No, you can't go." That's you in your feelings. Stay logical by saying: "Not today, baby, the sitter is tired. You wore her out. We'll try again tomorrow or the next day." Now that's more like it. Why? The sitter may have had a rough day taking care of a *great* responsibility. The sitter probably failed another online test. While you were sitting at your desk working, the sitter was cleaning sugar off the kitchen floor. The babysitter is sometimes more emotional than logical, and some don't realize the difference between them. Relax, this is the way life works. Every day wasn't like yesterday, but every day is perfect.

Tip #14: There are two types of parents. The first type has genuinely never looked at the tips in this manner. They will keep these tips in mind, which will help them better in the future. The other type of parent loves to see the sitter sitting at home keeping multiple babies. If this parent had anything to do with it, they would lock the sitter up and throw away the key. Well, I have news for this parent: Cinderella escaped.

Tip # 15:

1) Consider this your parental help manual before, during, and after you build a lovely family.

2) You don't have to be old to be wise. You must listen and pay attention.

3) Don't be too shy to ask someone you trust to help you on your journey. If you approach your sitter in a way that will benefit you both, she'll consider. Imagine this discussion and try it if you need to: "Ms. Applesauce, thank you for all you've done for me and my family. We couldn't do what we do without you." Pause. If she has something to say, let her speak. Then continue, "You are part of our family; I trust you. You know you can't trust everybody nowadays." Ha ha ha, you two will probably snicker a tad bit here. Continue, "I need you on our team. I've been offered a great opportunity, and I would love for you to be the one I patronize. You set your price no matter what it is, but here's what I need, and then you give me your quote." Now, tell her what time you're going to drop them off, pick them up, etcetera. If you conduct your offer in a loving way, she'll help you. Once you get what you need, make it your vow to

check on her at least one day a week. Set your timer for ten minutes 😊 and make time for the lady who made your visions tangible. Your kids are going to grow up, and you never want to be labeled "you forgot where you came from."

4) Be real with yourself. If you love to work, make sure you have a great career to pay for daycare.

5) If for any reason you are not sure, honestly, wait on the Lord. Now this could mean months, even a year or two, but wait.

6) Remember to play the what-if game. After you've finished this chapter, put your hand on your chest, state your name, and say, "In all thy ways acknowledge him, and he shall direct thy path" (Prov. 3:6 KJV).

Remember: this chapter is to help stretch your thinking, and when someone tells you you'll never be ready for a baby, you can say, "If I try, I can be better prepared."

CHAPTER 9
Misunderstanding and Illness

I was back at home, in the kitchen looking like Clair Huxtable—as my husband described me—with my heels on frying chicken, whipping cornbread, and stirring my black-eyed peas. The "Real Housewife of Coldspring." As the day moved late into the evening, I decided to shower and hit the sack early. All of a sudden, God said, "Teacher Goffney."

I jumped out of the shower, barely dried off, got dressed, ran into the living room, and told my husband, "God wants me to go back to college to be a schoolteacher!"

He smiled and bucked his eyes. "That's great, sweetie." We both cheered! He let me carry on and on.

The next day I hurried and made an appointment to speak with an advisor with what I thought I understood. After arriving on campus and sitting for twenty minutes, "Roberta Goffney," I jumped up (like I hit the lottery) and walked, switching, into her office. She explained I needed quite a few hours to complete my bachelor's degree in teaching. I listened to what she said, but the disappointment concerning the time for completion numbed me. Nevertheless, "Teacher Goffney" echoed on the inside of me. Because of the resounding, I followed through.

I got over what the advisor said and focused on what I believed God said. I took the necessary steps to enroll in college. It had been so long since I attended school, the admission office needed up-to-date paperwork. I traveled to Houston, Texas, and waited in line for six hours. Then I drove back to Conroe to turn in one document. Really? What a challenge. I didn't give up. I continued praying to God. "God, I'm aware you said 'Teacher Goffney.' I need to register for the class. Help me, Lord."

After a couple of days of the hustle and bustle, the college completed the paperwork, and I registered for classes. Swoosh, what a relief. Thank you, Lord.

The following spring semester of 2013, our professor assigned a class project. Every student had to show what the display insinuated, and the audience would only see pictures. When the professor peeked inside my maze, she saw one woman doing several different duties.

In the first section of the labyrinth, the woman had on an apron standing in front of the stove. Second, she fed her baby in the highchair. Third, she helped her children with their homework. Fourth, she laughed with family and friends. Fifth, she sat at her desk as an employee. Sixth, she was an entrepreneur. And seventh, she was slow dragging (dancing) with her husband. Wow! The image hit me. That's an All-in-One Woman. She's mastering multiple duties and has found joy in them despite her past.

After that fun day of learning, I maintained a busy life and enjoyed the classes; however, I admit the responsibilities became annoying. Yes, I had this. Many days, my energy level mastered unstoppable. But then seventy-two hours later, I wondered, was I supposed to be stretched this far? Like I didn't have enough to do, considering Santavia would graduate that May of 2013. Sanshae was eleven and active in school. Anything she participated in, she enjoyed. Shani'ya was seven, and Shantel was five. I was taking care of my wife's duties and my side hustles. Is this how my life's supposed to be?

As time rocked on, I dug deeper. I honestly asked myself why I was striving for a four-plus year degree when I was not planning on clocking in and out as an employee. I clocked in and out every day working for my family. God didn't create me for the pressure I applied to myself. From observation, teachers couldn't be teachers. Many stressed over the students passing the State Test instead of being a teacher—like the good old days, in the late '70s and early '80s. I lost my zeal for teaching in the school district.

"God, I heard you; however, I have no desire to teach school anymore. I desired to walk across the stage as a college graduate since I missed the opportunity in high school." God didn't reply. "Teacher Goffney" continued ringing on the inside of me. I cried, pleading with God to talk to me. No answer. From my experience, when God doesn't answer, do not move. A couple of days passed, and I contacted my forever friend. She explained to me that God chose me as a teacher in the ministry. "No, he did not, friend!" She chuckled, so did I. A couple of minutes of laughing, tears forming in my eyes, and all jokes aside, we continued in a serious conversation.

With purity in her eye, she told me, "You are part of the five-fold ministry. That's what God meant."

"Really? Where is that again in the Bible?" (Look at me, acting like doubting Thomas.) I listened to what she said. "And he gave some, apostles; and some, prophets; and some, evangelists; and some, pastors and teachers" (Eph. 4:11 KJV).

After we parted, I talked with God. "God, is this true?" No answer. I cried. Was I worthy of such a gift? Not from my view. I figured; he's not talking to me. I guess "Teacher Goffney" reckons to finish college to be a schoolteacher. So, I carried on.

A few months later, after all that intense information, we were informed my dad had colon cancer. That was heartbreaking news. Just when life seemed decent, now this? My dad and I were not close, but we were not distant either. No matter what, that was my daddy, and I loved him.

Once I got married and had four daughters of my own, I better understood what being a spouse meant. Walking away from a marriage was easier than staying. Sometimes, the individual's needs trump the couple's needs. My husband encouraged me to spend as much time with my dad as possible, and I did.

I drove him to his doctor appointments in Lufkin, Texas. My dad was such a private man, he didn't verbally say what was on his mind, though he spoke volume with his looks. Me being me, I loved getting an understanding, and I wanted to hear his side of the story. What happened between him and Mom when I was a little girl? I was *full* of questions. But I took the hint—he wasn't full of answers. The expression on his face and his body language spoke more than words. So I decided to leave the past in the past. Besides, he was stubborn most of the time, and I was stubborn some of the time. We made the best of our time while we had the chance.

After Dad's doctor's appointment, we drove to Sonic. He enjoyed a peanut butter shake with his lunch. "My, my, my, that's my favorite."

Looking at dad with enjoyment, I said, "Oh, where are the salty fries? Goodness, that's delicious."

He didn't eat many potatoes; he wanted peanuts with our shake. He got tongue-tied, "Give me 15, 22, 25 of those peanuts, Bert."

I almost choked. Eyes bucked, loving the moment to the fullest, I said, "You want 15, 22, 25, peanuts? W.T.!"

Eventually, Dad got to a point where he didn't want to go to Sonic after the doctor visits. He said to me one day, "Bert, why do I feel like they are killing me when they are supposed to be healing me?"

"Well, Daddy, I've been told that's what the medicine does when you have cancer."

He didn't like the torture of the needles and decided the best thing to do was to stop taking the medicine. He frustrated me to the core; I needed him healed. I didn't say much after I noticed how irritated the discussion made him, but I can't say I was happy about his decision. I tried everything in my power to persuade him to continue treatment. I even suggested he try the pill. He was so stubborn at times. Nevertheless, we enjoyed each other's company from that day forward as much as we could. When I would drop him off at home, I immensely thanked my aunt for taking care of my dad as long as she had.

As time ticked on, my dad's health decreased, not to mention our oldest daughter just graduated in May of 2013, and the spring semester of college ended for me.

Distractions were all around me. I couldn't focus on anything. My dad's health condition gave me a reason to pursue a job to help with expenses. If I found something close to home, it would benefit the entire family. My husband wouldn't understand, but the decision would be best for the family. Guess what? My new occupation was close to home, a hop, skip, and a jump. Although I didn't plan to stay on this job, I enjoyed the stay immensely.

Life was perfect. The season was a delicate time for the entire family. I realized working and going to college at the same time may not be a good idea. Therefore, that summer semester, I didn't return to college. In the weirdest way, life was still perfect. I enjoyed my family, my dad, and my friends to the fullest. It was like back in the old days—a loving family.

As time rocked on, it was one bad thing after another. Santavia wrecked another car, causing our car insurance to increase to $600 a month. The dryer quit working; we thought it was the heating element. Unfortunately, we had to replace it. I couldn't understand how something so right turned so wrong.

God used my own words on me: "I'll show you better than I can tell you." I had countless nights of unrest.

The chasing was unpeaceful. My marriage took a turn, our finances took a turn. Life was so congested, I wanted to get a divorce. Yes, it had gotten that dreadful. When my forever friend called to check on me, I went off on her. "Don't pray for me! I need a friend right now, not a minister!" The season was unexplainable. When Sissy called, she tried comforting me. It worked for a minute or two, and then, click. I voiced a whole lot of foolish talk.

"Okay! I see you, God! This how your spankings work? I couldn't say yes when I wasn't sure."

One day I was home alone; Santavia and the girls were having a girls' day out. God, I heard what you said, but I have no desire to teach school anymore. As for the ministry, I do not want to hurt anyone's feelings, causing them to leave the church(s), not come around family, not participate in parties, not want to go to lunch. Everywhere I went, I was going to have to deal with "feelings." God, you will not let me rest. If you have chosen me, please prove it is you.

Instantly, I had a flashback of an episode at TDCJ

in the control picket years ago. I knew what the scripture meant; however, one of the officers thought differently and said, "Look at you, quoting the scripture, don't know where it is." Although the officer had his opinion, I ignored his words. Deep down inside I believed. However, I repented for the way I said it. When I spoke, it didn't always make a person comfortable. I apologized for my roughness, but the officer was adamant that I didn't apprehend the scripture. I was over the coworker's belief. I just wanted better for them as a human being, and that was understanding.

After the flashback, at the kitchen table, I had the Bible in front of me. As I was reading the scripture, this was what came to me: That which matters to you, you hold it close to you. The *matt* in matter is the same *matt* in the book of Matthew. Five plus one is six. Matthew 5:16 KJV says, "Let your light so shine before men that they see your good works and glorify your Father which is in heaven." Tears flowing from my eyes and snot running out my nose, I boohooed for a while. I could not get it together. I never in my life heeded to such a sound. There is *no way* I could have thought of the scripture in that fashion. Not me.

God knew my heart. I needed assurance that it was him "choosing" me in the ministry. Was it clear! You better know it was! I didn't need any more proof.

Thank you, God, for confirmation. As many souls as we can reach, I'm willing. That day I accepted my calling as "Teacher Goffney" in the ministry.

CHAPTER 10
Teacher in the Ministry

After a few days of accepting my calling in the ministry, I informed my pastor what God had told me to do for His Kingdom's work. Despite what I didn't want to do in the beginning and butterflies in my tummy, I knew everything would be okay.

One day I went walking through the trail in my community—me, God, and nature. The Lord began to reveal to me my understanding of the church. He showed me a whole lot in one hour of exercise. For the most part, I tried to keep a positive attitude in the house of worship, no matter what. I loved going to church and still love attending. My church family had been a blessing for years. We didn't visit each other much, but when we did come together to rejoice and lift the name of Jesus with extended family, the occasion was a blessing. Especially special occasions; for example, every February, one of our ministers gave Bishop a musical, and different groups came and sang an A and B selection. OMG, talk about the talented voices in the church—all ages were in the *house*! "Y'all better sang!" Talk about a good time, oh yeah. A mighty-mighty good time.

Another unforgettable moment: the youth matrons and several parents volunteered to take the children to a resort overnight. This trip was the children's all-time favorite. We slept in a cabin built over a swamp, and if you walked on the balcony, you could see the alligators. Gosh, the children loved it. You all know I was a little afraid. Hahaha. But the experience was well worth it. I got over my feelings and enjoyed the moment. We always had a blast when we took our youth department on field trips.

And, oh child, how about the churches in surrounding areas. I cherished the moment when everyone in one building gave God the worship and praise and lifted the name of Jesus. What's not to love about that? And let me not forget, witnessing loved ones walk to the altar to be saved. Hallelujah! Who wouldn't celebrate!

But let's move forward in the church. After the praise and worship were over and it was time for God's word, the preacher took his stand at the podium to bring the scripture. Uh oh. His performance started out smooth, calm, and collected.

The minister gave reverence to God (definitely the right thing to do), acknowledged other ministers on the roster, respected the spouse, and lastly, recognized the whole household of faith. In other words, he warmed up. He continued in his message that the scripture "cut like a two-edged sword," and what a look on his face! In those days, preachers didn't manage their facial expressions; in their defense, I don't believe they realized how they looked, "cared" how their face appeared, or had anyone to bring it to their attention that they had a facial problem. You see . . .

I understood a lot of times what the preacher meant and their hyper-energy in their message. However, some folks in the congregation were like, "Huh?" The looks on their faces in the assembly were off the chain. As the minister preached like he had ants in his pants, he didn't realize the wicked spirit had confused the atmosphere through facial expressions. Facial expressions are a trick of the devil. The devil loved confusion then and loves turmoil now. I picked up on this early. How? From my own life experiences from my past. Remember, I was the girl who didn't always say it right, nor did it right, but honestly, I didn't mean any harm. I had a raspy voice, and when the word got good to me and the spirit took over, I got ugly at times and probably danced like I had ants in my pants. I'm sure the ushers had the white sheet ready to throw over me. The spirit will do that to you. Real talk. The touch is like "fire!" But several folks didn't understand. And if a person does not master this, the enemy will use facial expressions as a weapon. And be careful, you can't remember the importance of God's message thinking about how the preacher looked at you. Hint: that's a trick of the enemy.

Therefore, I tried my best to smile and pray at the same time. Lord, please rest the spirit of a smile on the preacher's face to alert him/her that the enemy is on his job, confusing folks. Nevertheless, I understood how the preacher felt. So I kept smiling. In the preacher's defense, he or she only wanted what's best for humanity, for us to "repent for the kingdom of

Heaven is at hand" (Matt. 3:2 KJV). My goal stood firm in recruiting for the kingdom of heaven as a minister. And I believed many ministers encouraged others to repent, accept Christ as savior, walk in the water to be baptized for their sins' remission, in Jesus's name, amen. And from there, try. If I sensed the preacher was off task, I prayed for them. But I never made it about me. Satan's goal was and is to destroy the churches. It's been spiritual warfare before 1972 and will forever be spiritual warfare.

It was not, nor is it, the preachers' fault how an individual's relationship turns out with the Lord.

I wasn't responsible for how people treated me, but I was responsible for how I treated people. I tried to stay positive in every way. When I didn't remain optimistic, little hiccups like that caused me not to grow spiritually.

It didn't bother me one bit when the preacher(s) were preaching, and all of a sudden, they began talking about tight dresses. The root of me understood what they were saying. Although my dress may have been fitting, they were not talking to me. Why? I had a husband, and if I kept my husband looking at me, I didn't have to worry about him looking at anyone else.

The church was to help me stay close to God; my skirt was to keep me close to my husband.

Another situation: I couldn't understand why so many people in the church kept saying they were not perfect. It hit me: that's one way many pacified their mistakes, and others would excuse them. If we made a mistake, we made a mistake. I shrugged my shoulders and confessed I messed up. My hiccups gave the next person a chance to witness God's deliverance.

I said I was not perfect in the past too. Why did I say that when I believed all my life growing up that I could be? My granny sowed that into me: "Practice makes perfect." Think about this: we take out the trash, wipe, flush, pull up our bottoms, and wash our hands daily. Is that not perfection? On the flip side, as soon as some made a mistake, many grabbed that "crutch." Let the crutch go. Ask. God will forgive.

Here's the truth for several: "I don't like them; I don't speak to them." Well, your speaking may convince someone not to commit suicide. You might give someone "unspeakable" joy—just by waving. And not to mention, you let your little light shine.

So here's my proof you can be "perfect": "Be ye

therefore perfect even as your Father which is in Heaven is perfect" (Matt. 5:48 KJV).

The explanation of this scripture is this: grow and mature as human beings.

What I discovered is, people are perfect in that they want to be perfect in.

For those who have a habit of saying no one's perfect but Jesus, please note he didn't say try to be like him. He knows we can't be born from a Virgin Mary. He said, "Be like your father in Heaven." I understand. Old habits are hard to break, but you can do it. Once you come in the knowledge of the truth, transform. If you need a little help, fast and pray. Trust me: the two together is like dyno-mite. One can't help but discern a change in you. Don't make salvation hard. You are more than welcome to speak for yourself, but not "everyone" thinks the same.

God will *never* give human beings an assignment beyond our human capabilities.

One evening my cousin giggled nonstop; he barely got the words out: "I know God is real, Shelett. I remember the old you. Do you still do the splits?" His reminder didn't bother me one bit about my past. Why? I loved being an example of broken down for

God to pick up. We reminisced, laughed that day, and enjoyed the moment. He couldn't stop. I thought he was going to crack a rib laughing so hard. Suppose that was a way to recruit for the Kingdom. So be it. Have your way, Lord.

I've heard people say that when folk "act" a certain way in public, sweet, kind, or gentle, and then arrive home or elsewhere and act differently, they're "fake." I don't think that's fake. How can it be, unless the woman is a manikin? I am supposed to obey the scripture and let my light shine: "Let your light so shine before men, that they may see your good works, and glorify your Father which is in Heaven" (Matt. 5:16 KJV). Do you see the difference? That wasn't fake; it was obedience. I knew how to be a lady in the streets. However, at home, that's my palace. I helped build it. And think about this for a minute: do you think women in other countries worry about people calling them fake because they are obedient? They are trying to live. Some of their punishments are beyond what we know. The misunderstanding: our God was and is so good to us that some do not understand when he commands, "Let your light shine." We have so much freedom, that several have turned their light off, confused about what obedience means.

I overheard peoples' conversation: "I'm catching hell." I thought, well, that's the problem. I don't want anything that belongs to the devil. I have trouble sometimes, but God gave me the power to put little fires out. When the flame gets too big for me, I call my brothers and sisters in Christ. If they are unavailable, I call on my Heavenly Father. I learned the hard way. Power is in my tongue.

In hindsight, the way I interacted with a person about how they made me feel while they were in the pulpit or even in the congregation was not detrimental, as some made it seem. I've always believed in talking to a person to get an understanding. Not to cause a fight, but to clear the air. I never understood why so many believed in letting it go when it was so much easier to talk about it and get closure. There was something down on the inside that nudged me to get an understanding. God didn't want me walking around miserable about how someone made me feel yesterday. Even preachers would say to me, leave it alone. Why, if I was unhappy and didn't have clarity? Therefore, I would call the person off to the side, just them and me, to reconcile the situation. That's all I needed to do. And guess what? I did the right thing. The person(s) and I were at peace, and even laughed at times. Low and behold, there is scripture to support my actions, "Moreover if thy brother shall trespass against thee, go and tell him his fault between thee and him alone: if he shall hear thee, thou hast gained thy brother" (Matt. 18:15 KJV).

I believe in my heart if people would learn how to communicate, we would have more time to rejoice than reject.

After God revealed this to me, I made a promise: I wouldn't let the enemy confuse people if I could help. With that said, on April 11, 2015, I delivered God's message with no paper. It was my voice used by the Holy Ghost:

The matt in matter is the same matt in the book of Matthew. Five plus one is six. Matthew 5:16 (KJV) tells us, "Let your light so shine before men, that they may see your good works, and glorify your Father which is in heaven."

That which matters to you, you hold it close to you.

The matt in matter is the same matt in the book of Matthew. God gave me five fingers on the right hand so I could wave and say hello. Four plus four is eight. Matthew 5:48 (KJV) says, "Be ye therefore perfect, even as your Father which is in heaven, is perfect."

My baby brother's nickname was Duke. It rhymes with Luke. I was fifteen when he passed in May of 1988. He was ten years old. Luke 15:10 (KJV) says, "Likewise, I say unto you, there is joy in the presence of the angels of God over one sinner that repenteth."

The e in evil is the same E in the book of Ephesians. In grade school, we learned that 6 + 6 = 12. Ephesians 6:12 KJV says, "For we wrestle not against flesh and blood but against principalities, against powers, against the rulers of the darkness of this world against spiritual wickedness in high places."

A few times, when I acted a monkey, my spirit had to jerk my flesh by the collar. The jer in jerk is the same jer in the book of Jeremiah. Jeremiah 32:27 (KJV) says, "Behold, I am the LORD, the God of all flesh: is there anything too hard for me?"

"Ouch! No, sir." I repented, cried, straightened up, and got it right.

I had never witnessed the Holy Ghost in such a way. I'd been chosen. I sensed everyone in the congregation believed in God that night. God did it again: proved himself to me and others.

Remember me telling you my dad had colon cancer in the previous chapter? Well, after that blessed night, I spent every day possible with him. I prayed to God for my dad's peace while he was in the land of the living. I enjoyed every minute in the Woodlands with him. Sickness limited his days on earth with his family. Luke 15:10 nested on the inside of me, giving me peace about what was about to come. My dad was in God's hand. The devil could *only* do what God let him do . . . nothing. I said, "God, when you do it, I know it's done. He's in your hand." On May 29, 2015, my dad Willie Dave Thompson Sr. was absent from the body to be present with the Lord (2 Cor. 5:8).

Little brother, Willie Dave Thompson Jr., give Dad a tour of the city that we can only imagine on earth. RIP, Daddy.

Thank you, Jesus.

CHAPTER 11
The Power of Change

After my dad passed, my reasons for working in the workplace changed drastically. Unaware of how the job was going to play out, my position that God granted in 1999 to be a wife and a mother waited for me. I knew giving a two weeks' notice was out of the question. I let time take care of itself and enjoyed life with my family, friends, business associates, and coworkers until 2015 ended.

Life journeyed on as normal, New Year's, work, Valentine's Day, St. Patrick's Day, and birthday parties; Mother's Day, Father's Day, anniversaries, sports, clubs, church—you name it, we did it.

Summer of 2016 arrived, and my husband drove his family to Florida. Yes, yes, yes! We had sixteen hours' worth of drive time, which gave me time to think when the girls went to sleep, and Honey listened to his "Lee William's" CD.

Prior to this vacation, I saved coins—as a goal—for the trip; the silver purchased the gas to Florida and back to Texas. Although the girls didn't like summer schoolwork, we had fun counting a few of the quarters. Why not? How many children comprehend how many quarters are in a roll? And how many rolls did it take to drive to Florida and back to Texas? Let's just say, cha-ching! Throughout the ride, we stopped at least twenty times. "Goodness. You have to use the ladies' room again, Mama?" baby girl asked while clowning and having fun in the back seat. My anxiety level went sky high. Although the best Uber driver in the world drove, the thought of crossing the bridge in Louisiana terrified me. I got over it, though; I looked forward to the magical moment. There was power in change. I believed anyone could travel to Disney by consistently saving *cha-ching*!

"Walt Disney World, here we come!"

Our family loved our vacations. Down through the

years, if we did nothing else, we were going to recuperate. Considering five of us traveled together, we always drove. My babies were with me, we packed what we wanted to take, and we stayed as long as we wanted to.

"Whoo-hoo!!! Let's party, babies!"

"Everybody but the driver throw your hands in the air!"

"Ain't no party like a Goffney party, 'cause a Goffney party don't stop . . ."

Once we got to the hotel and settled in, we headed to the theme park.

"Wow . . . I hope everyone experiences a magical moment."

On the way back, the girls slept most of the way, and Honey nodded. I had nothing but time to think. Granny was right about keeping a clean house. I didn't change what she sowed into me, but I enhanced it. If I didn't have time to clean, I'd pay someone. Cleaning all day is a distraction. Changing some of the ways I handled my duties was okay. My change didn't have to be complete; an enhancement would do just fine.

Our Disney World ended, wonk, wonk, wonk. And back to work we went.

At this point, I realized God had used me for an escape for someone else to leave the workplace. Sometimes people hate to leave a company they've been so loyal to. But how will one taste the greatness that waits for them if they never *change* positions? Through that experience, I discovered it was comforting for coworkers to know if they left the job, but I was there, I'd continue the work they taught me. No worries, I got your back, Sis.

Once the assignment was over, I waited patiently. That same year, a lady approached me about a position from a different place of employment. You know me, yep, excited. This new occupation was the answer to my escape. I was honored by what she saw in me. She said, "You're the woman for the job." Guess what? I took the position.

Although I was honored to transition to another place of employment, I hated to leave my previous work family, but I had to move on.

I didn't know how long I would be at the new assignment, but I went with the flow. I could see God moving.

August 2017, I had been on the new job for eight months, when Hurricane Harvey landed in Houston,

Texas. The time I spent with my loved ones witnessing the sad moments of other families on the news losing their relatives because of the disaster, helped me conclude my decision. But I had to follow God's lead. The time had come. I prayed, paused, and reflected. I didn't have to work in a stressful environment when my personality said otherwise. I confessed what I needed; and stress wasn't what I needed. One day I wanted to walk out the door and leave! Daily, on the job, it blew my mind how people could not activate their power in happiness. My spirit tugged on me.

"Whose fault is it you're in this situation?"

"Ouch. Mine."

"Then wait until the Lord delivers you. Maybe this time you'll learn to balance."

As time rocked on, one day I did my makeup, talking to God as usual. "God, I don't want to be busy all the time." Some days I noticed I'd be all over the place, unable to focus. It hit me. I stopped and looked closer in the mirror; God showed me that distraction to my focus was like a blink of an eye. That changed my world. I viewed distractions in a whole new light and became more aware by paying attention to a faint blink.

After Hurricane Harvey ended, I traveled to talk to an advisor at Lone Star College in December 2017. We went over the classes I had to complete, and she explained, "If you stay consistent for the rest of 2018, you can graduate in the fall." The high school teenager in me jumped and shouted! It was one of the happiest days of my life. YES! I cheesed from ear to ear. You couldn't tell me nothing!

I had to focus, and balance.

May 2018, I came home with no regrets, not worried, distracted, unbalanced, miserable, or unsure, but 100 percent certain, proud, balanced, focused, peaceful, and back in college full time. I was ready to "just be…"

College was in session…

As time passed one evening after class, traffic stopped. An accident must have happened. I couldn't see ahead, and I wondered what was going on. Traffic must have been twelve cars deep. On a pleasant note, sitting in traffic helped me put some things in perspective. My spreadsheet became a bit easier. But I couldn't get over the voices of some who said, "the poor, the middle class, and the rich." Considering that phrase, I thought, "The middle class isn't too bad." If a person or couple had $999,999, they weren't rich, but they were not poor. Some would consider that middle class; a few would say that's plenty; others, more than enough; others, that's change. I learned it depends on whose purse it's in. Has anyone ever said to you, "Oh, I am so proud of you and your husband; y'all are doing so good for yourselves and your daughters"? You reply, "Thank you, we're blessed but . . ." " No buts, baby. Thank the Lord because many people want to be in your shoes. You and your husband have worked together, and now y'all own some things."

Or maybe a different group of people encourages you to do more. They may also be right. It just depends on their perspective. I knew many people viewed my situation differently. But I concluded it was okay. The middle isn't too bad.

I'm not the first to be born; I won't be the last. I will not be the first to live and will not be the last to die. When I think about the father, the Son, and the Holy Ghost, Jesus is in the middle.

CHAPTER 12
Amazing Husband Part 1

Although it took eighteen years and eleven months to calm down and realize I had a solid foundation in us, your patience was unbelievable. During our one year of dating, we joked about why we got married. But as time progressed, I'm glad we were able to be real with one another. You got married for love; I got married for the hanky-panky. Keeping it real, I trusted I was enough, and you didn't have to sleep with Ms. Pear and Sister Celery when you had steak at the house. Thank you, Mr. Goffney, for assuring me, I am all you need. Besides Beltway 8 and toll road 99, herpes, the clap, gonorrhea, and chlamydia, just to name a few, are the next things that scare the stuffing out of me.

I never wanted a long-term relationship with a penis I couldn't trust. For us, confession of why we united in Holy matrimony set us free. I've never been the woman who wanted to be married to say, "I'm married," or because a man hurt me, and I wanted to prove to him that I could have a husband. That frame of mind leads to divorce—at least for me it would have. You never have that to worry about. You being you, persuaded me. And for that, I'm grateful.

Once upon a time, we argued when you said, "You need a hookup." Now we laugh. I did need a hookup; I walked around nagging sometimes. It wasn't that my vitamin D was low, but my attitude needed adjusting. And you were the mechanic to fix that problem. Ha ha ha, but it's the truth.

Yes, marriage is definitely more than intimacy, but when I was real with myself, you didn't care if I cleaned the house, washed, or cooked. I put a lot of that on myself. I dug deep. If I was a single woman, which you made it clear I wasn't, I still would have cleaned, washed, etcetera. I've never had to pick up behind you. Truthfully, when I looked around, those were my shoes on the floor and clothes on the bed. I get it.

Life moved so fast that sometimes I didn't know

what to say or do. Our babies were attached to my umbilical cord for nine months, and I had the free leche. Now I see. When we had our daughters if I would have said, "Honey, you may consider working at Walmart a few nights to stock shelves because your income right now is not enough," being the man you were, you would have attempted it. But me striving to help you fogged that thought. I witness how tired you were pushing to do good behind the scenes for your family and others. You were the type of man who did what naturally made sense. But being a team player, I didn't want you scarring your elbows alone. You massaged my shoulders; I massaged yours.

One of us had to support the girls on game nights. You're correct; it made sense for it to be me. I see your point.

I'm delighted that God joined us together and we didn't sync ourselves. If I hadn't dated other guys in the past, I might not have appreciated you. That's why dating is important to me. Prepare yourself; our girls are going to have to date. And it may be more than one fellow. Don't worry. We've taught them right; dating doesn't mean sleeping with the dude. Our daughters have common sense to make moral decisions.

Thank you for taking over the dividend stock section of the spreadsheet. I told you—you would figure it out quicker than I could. Ha ha ha. It took us awhile, but we figured it out. Our girls couldn't understand when we expressed, we were no longer paying $600 a month in car insurance, which occurred after our oldest girl wrecked three cars, causing the coverage to increase. So, we kept driving Dalmatian and keep driving Dalmatian, which was our ugly white car with chipped paint. We understood that we should invest $300 in dividend stock and the other $300 budgeting the weekends for them. They thought they were big shots. And you know what—they were, but only because of the decisions we made. We know our goals and visions, and with that said, there's nothing that *time* can't bring. According to one of our family members, "Rubber on wheels beats rubber on heals."

Yes. We've had our ups and downs, but we're in it to win it until death do us part. And I pray we'll be so old if one of us perishes before the other that we'll have enough memories to keep us moving. You are such a wise man. Keep doing what you're doing, Mr. Goffney—living the Life.

Amazing Husband Part 2

Your treatment was my kryptonite.
It helped me realize
That where I was weak,
You were strong, that helped our love survive.
When you were out all day, I couldn't breathe.
Without you period, I couldn't live.
Your words have never harmed me.
And your arms have always embraced me.
Your 2:30 a.m. was intriguing,
Staying consistent in taking care of your family.
When I threatened to leave, your eyes asked,
"Why?"
Stretching my mind to think
A lot of times, I wanted to hear your voice
Missing the signal in a sigh.
What was a woman to do?
Coming across a man like you,
Unsure if you were real?
But I took a chance, not in romance,
To see what you would do.

You proved yourself in action form
That spoke louder than words could say.
We didn't know if we were wrong or right,
But the one thing you believed: wait on God's eyesight.
My impatient self couldn't wait;
Even being wrong, you took the bait.
Remember that time we drove far, far away?
That one memory will never get displayed.
We laughed, joked, snickered the whole ride,
Pleading with the Lord to close his eyes.
We learned to live Holy; it took a little time,
Two young kids growing side by side.
One of your strengths
You didn't sweat the small stuff,
Proving to me I was more than enough.
You loved me like God loved the church.
And I loved you more than the fish loved the water.
Thank you, Mr. Goffney, for you being you,
There will never be another who can do what you do.

CHAPTER 13
Dazzling Daughters

Corn grows tall, cotton thick, the way I love my babies makes the old folks sick.

I could get ahead of myself by saying, being a mother was an experience I wouldn't change for the world. It is a book in itself. In the beginning, it was overwhelming, especially since it didn't come naturally for me. I had no idea raising four girls was that challenging.

When I was a child, I had visions of being a schoolteacher, a cheerleader, an actress, a track star, a famous woman (like Ms. Kitty on Gun Smoke) or meeting the wrestler Junkyard Dog. Those were the visions I had. Can I keep it real? I never envisioned being a wife nor a mother. You see, the young girl in the woman was naturally outgoing. All I had were great visions. I knew who I wanted to be, but not who I was going to be. My future was not visible. Back in the day, the only time I was a mother was when we played the "mash." We took a piece of paper in four sections, and on the inside, it revealed I was married, had four kids, and drove a Ferrari. Why a two-seater? I had no idea with four children and a husband. But that was a game, and my make-believe teacher's name was Ms. Carter.

Other than that, my vision(s) was not about settling down. People, people, and more people, I loved people. That is as clear as my future was back in the day. But as I fast-forward into motherhood at the beginning, I was horrible. I cried one moment and laughed the next. There were many days and nights I asked myself, "What happened? How did this responsibility slip up on me like this?" The skill of motherhood didn't come naturally for me. I had to work at it over and over again. Although I bumped my coconut multiple times, I was always able to have joy in it. I had help when I needed it. My mom, in-laws, family, and friends would step in when I needed help. I was so grateful for them.

On the other hand, when those babies were sick,

vomiting, crying, you name it, I had to do it. My babies wanted their mama. This responsibility was not one you do in forty-eight hours, and it is over. But understanding that I loved my babies and my husband helped me push through the unanswered questions. My responsibility as a mother kept me sane. The peace of their little heartbeats would melt my soul. When I held each of them in my lap, rocking them to sleep, I knew just from the love of their little heartbeats I was doing the right thing. When times became overwhelming, I thought about the old folks saying, "Practice makes perfect." This cliché stuck with me.

Some days I would speak into the atmosphere, "Lord, I do not know what I am doing. I have never been a mother of four before." In the nick of time, while we were out and about, a woman would say, "They grow up so fast. Hug and kiss them as much as you can. They'll be grown and out of your house before you know it." When I heard that, I was like, "Are they talking to me?" I needed those words. I didn't get it then, but it was true. I thought that duty was going to last forever. If I had to do it all over again, I definitely would. But this time, I wouldn't seek after corporate America. I had corporate: being a wife, mother, and me.

As a child growing up, I would always keep my sister's girls, and as soon as I found out she was expecting another child, I would ask her, "Don't you know what causes that!" I could always give her kids back. I never had to keep them 24/7, 365 days of the year. Once I had my four girls, she asked me, "Don't you know what causes that?" (Ouch, I reaped what I sowed.) I thought, "Submission?"

Thank you, my four beautiful daughters, for allowing me to be your mother. For your encouragement, space, and cheering me on to do this for you and generations to come. I pray the inheritance that I have instilled in you, you will instill in your children.

I pray that I have taught you to love the Lord God with all your hearts first. Secondly, your family. Thirdly, it is your choice, keep it Holy. You all are free to make your own decisions. I am at peace when I know you are saved. I have built a team. "No matter what, you girls stick together." I do not have a crystal ball, and I cannot say what's going to happen in the next ten minutes. Stay balanced, and do not put outsiders before each other. If one is hungry, feed her. No matter how you think, feel, or believe, *know* that is your sister.

You girls have no idea how grateful I am to be your mother; I love you more than words can say. Being your mom has gotten more comfortable with time; you all are forever my sweethearts. If I had to start over, I would do it in a heartbeat. The only thing I would change is the diaper stage. Hahaha.

Santavia

Santavia, my beautiful firstborn, had the nurse side of me. I loved taking care of people when they were sick; however, she was all in for real. She liked the wombs and all—not my department. I'll never forget the day Santavia asked me for a dollar. Remember, she's the kid who loved to do everything. She was the one who had me ripping and running nonstop. I said, "Sweetie, mommy doesn't have a dollar right now." The look on her face followed the words coming out of her mouth, looking at me from head to toe, "You don't have a dollar?" Like, you're all dressed up looking cute and don't have one dollar? "Get it off your credit card 'cause I know you have a bunch of dollars." Santavia, it was and is a privilege being your mom. Thank you for the hip name, *glamma*. I absolutely love it. You and my son-in-law have done an amazing job together…

Son-in-law, I love you to the core. Thank you for all of the surprises behind the scenes, especially that homemade gift when you first joined the family. It's the little things that take me a long way. And most of all, thank you for taking care of your household. Witnessing you grow into manhood was ecstatic; you've proven there are still great men in the world, and I am so glad my daughter inherited a great man in you.

Jarvis Jr., Shanyira, S'kiya, and Selah, I wouldn't change being your glamma (grandmother) for anything in the world. My love for you is unexplainable. I understand now why my mom was so lenient on my children. Once you join the grandma club, you'll understand. Until then, love your grandparents on both sides while you have the chance. And continue to love God as he loves you, and everything will be just fine.

Dear Mom" :)

I want to start this letter with letting you know that I love you very much. Mom you are the best woman that god ever created, and I am so honored to have you as a mom, to Even though I don't show it as much as I should I want you to know that I love you so much. You picked a great husband I'm so glad he's my pops, instead of some dead beat ~~father~~ dad like my sperm donor (lol) =)... But daddy is a great man and I love him very much. I know that I may seem like I have an atitude & stuff, but I don't be meaning to. I know you have been 15 before so you should understand me when I tell you I really like ▮▮▮, & I think you should give a chance, he not the cutest thang in the world, but he is a real sweet down to earth person. I want to get closer to GOD, but I can't do it by myself. I need you to help me, cuz you may not know it, but I talk to him like he was my big brother and I be catching myself laughing like he was really there lol=) but I love the lord man. =) Yeah anyway I think you should give ▮▮▮ a chance. =) Ummmmm.... I'm not to sure how to close this letter cuz I can write for hours, I really like writing, but ~~before you~~ before I go I want you to know that god said "he will never leave you or forsake" you so keep going strong. =) I'm always here

And I love you so much, & I love being apart of this family.

Thanks for your time.

Sincerly
Sintaia

Sanshae

Sanshae, my beautiful second born, definitely inherited the business personality from me. One of my memorable moments with her was when she had us so scared a few years ago. We were on vacation in San Antonio, Texas. We went out to eat, and in the early hours of that morning around 3:00 a.m., our baby was vomiting so much, it was unreal. The first thing we thought was food poisoning. The entire vacation, we stayed in the hotel room. We waited a couple of days until she was able to ride in the car without throwing up. It was horrible. We prayed and prayed. God did it again. Thank you, Lord, for your healing power.

Sanshae, I am immensely proud of you. Whatever you choose to do in life, you're capable. You've proven yourself on multiple occasions, so I have no worries. Sanshae, it was and is an honor to be your mother. Keep God first, and you cannot help but be next.

Dear Momma,

On September 12, 2001 you gave me life. Momma, not only did you give me life, but you loved me and "For all those times you stood by me," I am forever grateful. I have not always been right; but "For all the wrong that you made right," I am who I am today, God filled and successful. Every time I would be sick and weak, you were my strength, for the times I could not pray "You were my voice when I couldn't speak." Momma you have inspired me to go and not only be successful, but to love my children God blesses me with." I was blessed because I was loved by you," Momma, "I am everything I am because you love me." Momma, I Love You.

Love,

Cc ♥

Shani'ya

Shani'ya, my third beautiful born, has that athlete side of me. Oh wee, I love me some track . . . lol. Let me say it correctly: I love track. One memorable moment I will never forget with you is the day we left the pacifier outside on the tricycle. I said, "Shani'ya are you going to get your pacifier, or are you going to leave it on the tricycle?"

"Leave it."

"Okay, if you leave it, we're not coming back to get it."

We went in the house. That night she cried all night long. I told her repeatedly, "You left it outside on the tricycle." I rocked her back and forth. Singing wasn't enough. It hurt me more than it hurt her. After three days of heartache and pain, we made it through. That was the end of the pacifier.

Shani'ya Goffney, keep excelling in you. You remind me a lot of myself. And one thing I know for sure is, if you can see it, you'll achieve it. It was and is a privilege being your Madre. Keep loving God. If he did it before, he will do it again.

Madre,

    I know we don't talk alot and when we do I talk your head off. I Love you Madre.

↓ ↓
♡ ♡

↓ ↓
♡ ♡

Shani'ya

Shantel

Beautiful Shantel. She definitely has that dancing side of me. She taught herself how to back flip. One of my most memorable moments, she never could say September. We'd ask Shantel, when her birthday was, and she'd say, "Sep-a-ma-tember."

We had her say it over and over again. She said it so much that she literally performed a backflip while saying it.

"Shantel, when's your birthday?"

"Sep-a-ma-tember!"

Shantel, it was and is a privilege being your mother. You are a great little cook, gymnast, nail tech and more. Whatever you want to do in your life, you got this. I love you, too, baby. Keep your hands in God's hand, and you can't be anything but victorious.

Roberta, it comes from the German, and it's meaning is "FAMOUS".

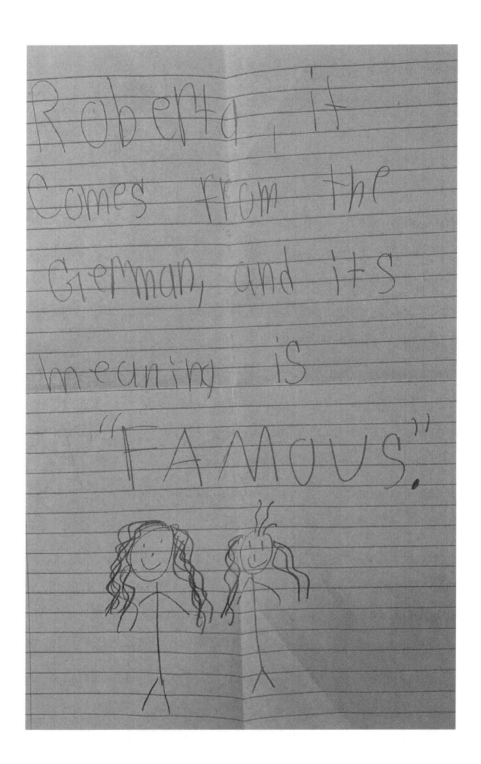

My mom is a good wife, good mother, great ceo. She will always be by your side. She will fight for you. She is **MY** ride or die. She is a very beautiful black lady. I love you mama.

CHAPTER 14
A Little "Peace" of Me

What Love Means to Me

No matter who you are, I respect you for being a human being. No matter how you look or smell, you are God's creation. Love, to me, is a simple act I will do for a person. I'll pray for you, feed you, give you something to drink, the list goes on. You mess up, I forgive you. You are human. And that's what makes you perfect to me. We may need to talk about some things, shed a few tears, but I *love* ya. Some folks are not going to understand like others, but I love them. Everywhere I go, I realize it's a soul.

Don't let foolish things separate you from people you are supposed to be connected to. My strength is knowing not everyone is in my group. Be real. I have four children; everyone can't be in my group. But I still love them.

If God loves his creatures, who am I not to?

Smart vs. Wise

When I was in grade school, I had some struggles. Certain peers were not as pleasant as others. Some made fun of me; they laughed and joked when I messed up or didn't know the answer. I didn't let that bother me. What they didn't realize was, that's how I learned. If one made a joke and it was on me, I figured it out. It took me a while to grasp the information, but once I understood, I shared my knowledge. Why? I learned in my life, I was not the brightest star in the sky, but I could be the sharpest tool in the shed. And when those who laughed witnessed how I helped others, they turned a different color. I was determined to remain educated.

Have you ever been in a class where the teacher asked a question, and all of a sudden, your classmate raised his/her hand quickly and the teacher called on them? The teacher calls on the student, and he/she gets the question correct, and you are like, wow, they are smart. I was like that once upon a time, but as I went to college and studied my own actions, I "solved the problem."

Let me show you what I'm talking about. When you can "solve problems," it makes you look "smart." You can look at it in different ways, just as long as you can solve the problem. For example, 5+5+5-12+8-6=? Is this smart or wise? Correct, it's smart. You solved the problem. If you are on the job in a meeting and a question is asked, and no one knows the answer but you because you are knowledgeable about the topic, is this wise or smart? I'm with you. I said both. You solved the problem; no one else knew the answer, and when you are knowledgeable about something, that's considered wisdom. The *know* that makes the word *know* is the same *know* that makes the word *knowledgeable*. A mom is in the kitchen preparing to scramble an egg. Her eleven-year-old daughter walks in without knowing how to scramble an egg, but she watches her mom do it. Is the daughter now smart or wise? Correct, wise, she now *knows* how to scramble an egg. Now that you are smart and wise, go get that promotion or start your own business. Always remember first things first: "In all thy ways ac*know*ledge him, and he shall direct thy paths" (Proverbs 3:6. KJV).

Dreamer or Visionary?

I had to be real with myself. Was I a dreamer or a visionary? Honestly, I got it. It sounds really good to say, "Follow your dreams," rather than, "Follow your visions." Has your mom or anyone ever said to you, "Get your head out of the clouds"? Or how about, "Quit that dreaming and go do what I told you to do!" Down through the years raising a family and making mistakes, I had to confess dreaming was not good for me. I was wide awake; life was real. My dreams were more of warnings. Some people were just that, daydreamers, but one must be a doer. Truthfully, when I dreamt at night, some of those dreams, I didn't want to come true. One day my oldest daughter said, "Mom, I had a dream you were having a baby."

"No thank you," I said with certainty. Even during the daytime, I didn't want to be a daydreamer. So, when I envisioned what I wanted to accomplish for me or my household, I set realistic goals. It is okay to dream. However, if you are the type that sits and stares into space, you need to quit dreaming. It's getting you nowhere. Be a "goal" digger, a visionary during the day. In other words, once you see what you want, while you are wide awake, then write your goals on paper, follow through, come back—review, believe, and achieve.

You Can Get Out . . .

Down through the years, I noticed how some women would act. And because of their actions, I would go to college to get educated. I didn't want women to feel like I was trying to take what was theirs. Take for instance, during a conversation, a woman's body language and look on her face said it all: I am not sharing this with Roberta; she might be better than I am if I teach her. I realized some women were not aware that college, universities, and businesspersons (entrepreneurs) encourage individuals to ask questions. In the women's defense, back in the day, people weren't encouraged to ask questions. If anything, many said, "Stay out of folks' business asking those questions." Therefore, my thoughts were: no worries, they are still learning who they are. So, to keep from asking, I would take a class in college to pay for my education.

Now there's YouTube. You know why? God fixed it because so many of us missed it looking for it; it's called *bartering*, which is an even exchange. For instance, back in the day, some folks had sugar and others had flour; they would make an equal trade. Swapping was common, and people believed in helping one another. Nowadays, you give a thumbs-up to the YouTuber and subscribe, and you receive free advice or entertainment. It was a win-win then and a win-win now. God made a way for his pure hearted.

If you are the type of person who thinks someone will take your idea, then shh or patent it. You are not wrong for patenting your idea. Reflect for a moment. There are many people who have had a "great" idea and patented their plan. On the contrary, learn the difference between being used by God and needing a patent.

I love giving information to help the next person be better. I knew I was never out to hurt anyone or take anything from others. However, paying for my education was easier, even if spending money was not always the right thing to do. Paying my way was more peaceful for me. This is why we have mentors in the world. A mentor has expertise in an area that helps others. We all must remember Proverbs 18:16 (NIV), "A gift opens the way and ushers the giver into the presence of the great."

If you are interested in going to college or graduate school, some require this as your first step. It's here if you need it. This form is the Free Application for Federal Student Aid (FAFSA). You never know where this first step will take you.

www.fafsa.ed.gov

Coworker Care

Party time! That's the great sound of employment. Everyone in the workplace has their reason for why they work and where they work. For me, it was meeting wonderful people, from the customers to the supervisors and coworkers. I still keep in touch with many of them, as genuine love is hard to let go. From learning multiple new tasks to giving a point of view on a particular topic, education is endless in the workplace. How about the food? Isn't it amazing how food brings people together? Parties of all sorts, birthdays, promotions, and retirement. Good times are contagious when you have a work family. Let me not forget the paycheck, health insurance, and retirement.

Viewing it from a different standpoint, I respect what some of you are thinking: it is not always a party on the job. Some days are more difficult than others. Absolutely, but on the other hand, power is given to you in how you control whatever is taking place. Take, for instance, if two of your coworkers are snickering and giggling in the cubicle next to you, as if you're not there, treating you a certain way in front of others, whether its customers, other coworkers, the manager, you name it. In their minds, they think they're putting you down or leaving you out. For me, I knew I didn't go there to stay. I kept my focus on why I was there: my paycheck, helping my customers, being friendly, letting my light shine, and going home. Honestly, that was my main reasoning for getting the job in the first place. I never planned on making it a career. For one, the employer could not pay me my net worth. I knew this. The coworkers, on the other hand, never knew my reasonings. At the time, I didn't think it was wrong for me to get a job to do great things for my children. It was never about me. That was my motive, but when women acted a certain way, I reflected on second grade. I quit making friends in second grade. I learned quickly that some girls thought I was going to take their friend from them. I was friendly with all my classmates. That experience encouraged me that if a girl is supposed to be my friend, a friend she will be. I've always loved everybody; if I continue this way, everyone will stay happy. Roots run deep. But some things on the earth never change; what happened in 1979 still happened in the '80s, '90s, and 2000s. Love anyway.

In hindsight—using my Holy Ghost imagination—I can hear God saying, "Okay. You do it your way, and I'll do it mine. I'll let them treat you like an outcast; I'll allow you to bring them closer for my glory." And that's exactly what happened.

With that said, if you've ever told God to use you, you are willing, and you're having trouble on the job, this might be your moment to be used by God. God using you is not going to always be in the form you are looking for. Stay positive, don't take the lesson personal; the All-Mighty may use you to bring them closer as friends or Christians or even deliver them. Whatever his will is, respect his doing. The coworkers may think you are the outcast, but God will show you. The results may not be instant, but you'll know. Just be the best you can be for the Kingdom. You are not responsible for how people treat you, but you are responsible for how you treat people.

Friends

I can get on the mountaintop and discuss this one. Before I get ahead of myself, I want you to understand *friend* is just a name to identify a person and who they are. Webster didn't say this. I'm saying it. Can a mentor be a friend? Sure they can. The relationship can start one way and end up another. Have you ever heard anyone say, "You're going to lose some friends along this way"? How about, "Some friends you just have to let go"? Or, "A real friend wouldn't do you like that"? Do any of these sound familiar? Let's dig deeper. What is it that makes people come up with quick, short phrases that seem right to say? Experience. Okay, I will take that. But this is why I went beyond the surface.

There are many reasons why people stop being "friends." Just to cover a few, most of the time there is no communication of what happened. Some people do not like confrontation, so it is easier just to let go. If one says this, the other says that, and it may start an argument, so they let it go with no understanding.

Let's go back to childhood. Has your mom ever asked you what's wrong with you? You reply that it's your friend, and your mom says, "Stay away from her. If she does not want to play with you, just stay away from her." That is exactly what you do. The question is, did your mom mean forever, just that evening, or a few days? Fast-forward to adulthood, sometimes some women might say to you, "Just don't say anything and leave her alone." But does the other woman mean forever, just that evening, or a few days? Sound familiar?

There were times when I was raising my children, going to college, or starting a new business, and I barely had time for my friends. Now keep in mind, I told you I love my friends, right? So, this is how I interact with them. There are some I do not see regularly, but we will send a quick *hello* text. I have a few I say hello to through quick e-mails or other social media platforms. There are *many* I see out and about if I have to go to the grocery store, the doctor, the gym, or wherever. It's always good to see my *girls* and hear from them when time allows. Then I have my friends who I interact with closely. They're very understanding of my life and vice versa. I have children and a husband, and they have children and husbands, so it's easier to have close friends like that. Now, because I am always educating myself, I have learned how to handle the relationship. Truthfully, this is not taught, but here you have it. "Friend, I thank you for cheering for me while I pursued my college journey, my hustle skills, my time with my family, or whatever you know I might be into . . . lol. You know I'm a "learn-a-holic." I'm getting schooled so I can come back and show you the ropes of how to." If I have to leave my friends, I come back to get them and share my wealth (information). Also, it's my passion to encourage them by asking questions which causes them to think.

You see, once upon a time, I didn't know my niche;

I had skills, but also I had a family. With that, even if it seems like my friends are moving too slow, I walk in understanding of what is holding them back. One may have to care for their sick parent, for example, so I try my best to assist as much as I can.

Some people do not know how to say, "I cannot help you right now, because I'm still trying to figure it out myself." During the time of them figuring it out, you drift apart. So, from this point on, when you hear someone say a phrase such as, "You're going to lose some friends along this way," "Some friends you just have to let go," or, "A real friend wouldn't do you like that" get to the core of what they are saying. Respect that but dig deeper. Stay positive. The truth is, for some it is easier to move on. The question is, was that ever your friend? Or did God just place that person in your life for you to help them and for them to help you? Sometimes the mission is for you to bless them. God may have moved them out of your way so he could reveal the good works in you. I've never lost a friend who was mine. For me, I know how to do friendly things. If a friend needs a friend, I'm a friend. Just remember, *friend* is a word that identifies the connection in a relationship. No, Webster didn't show me this. Understanding did.

A Letter to the Devil

When I think back over my life, I know I've made some mistakes, but there were some things I did right in God's sight. I write this section to the devil and all his kinfolk. It seemed like I was Pharaoh, but my heart has always been pure. You thought keeping me distracted would permanently make me lose focus. Devil, you thought keeping me in an ugly car was going to make me leave my family. Who does that, when they have the power to do more? You thought if you kept me "busy," I would never become productive. You thought because I managed, I would never become manageable? You believed because God didn't always answer, I would stop seeking him. You forgot that delaying me can't deny me. Anything I want is mine, considering I have the power to "ask." You thought, if I keep her in the middle, I can drag her to the end. Yeah, I was a little feisty; that was the power to put out your small fire. Devil, you thought if you kept me at a little, I'd never have a lot. I want to remind you if I can *teach* it, I definitely can live it!

You thought I had a Pharaoh moment, but you forgot about Job, devil. You've always been a lowercase.

Don't you dare remind me of what my parents didn't

do for me. What they didn't do, I had the power to do for me and for them. Now! Who missed it? I was determined to tell the whole world you are devious and manipulating and your favorite one of all, you loved and still love distractions. I rebuked you then, and I'm rebuking you now. In the name of Jesus! Now get back . . . I got work to do!

You Can't Hear God When . . .

You can't hear God when the devil is talking. What do I mean? When you're in the restroom all by yourself and a foolish thought comes to mind? Rebuke it. It's the devil. He loves misery. When your phone is always ringing and your notifications are always dinging, you can't hear God. The enemy will use everything he can to keep you distracted from God's will for your life. Remember, a distraction is to a focus like a blink is to the eye. Per Roberta Goffney.

God, I thank you that you are the only God who can edit, erase, plot, plan, and summarize my life with a permanent marker!

I am who you say I am: forgiven, powerful, and a woman!

Sometimes I'm sweet—other times I'm spicy.
Sometimes I teach—other times I'm the student.
Sometimes I'm hardheaded—other times I listen.
Sometimes I'm mean—other times I'm nice.
Sometimes I'm stuffed—other times I'm hungry.
Sometimes I'm skinny—other times I'm obese.
Sometimes I care—other times I don't at all.
Sometimes I'm private—other times I'm public.
Sometimes I'm the boss—other times I'm a flunky.
Sometimes I'm lonely—other times I'm entertained.
Sometimes I'm healthy—other times I'm ill.
Sometimes I ache—other times I'm pain-free.
Sometimes I'm rich—other times I'm poor.
Sometimes I'm clear—other times I'm confusing.
Sometimes I'm sure—other times I'm not.
Sometimes I'm charming—other times I'm hideous.
Sometimes I make mistakes—other times I'm perfect.
Sometimes I'm loved—other times I'm hated.
Sometimes I'm slow—other times I'm fast.
Sometimes I know—other times I know nothing.
Sometimes I'm flesh—other times I'm Spirit.
All the time—I'm a woman.

CHAPTER 15
Revealing the Greatness Within

December of 2018 was one of the happiest times of my life. I was able to spend some valuable time with my nieces, nephews, and nephew JB. All of them, from Coldspring to Corrigan, loved our house. They consider our crib the hangout. One of my sisters-in-law said, "It's Roberta's boot camp." Lol. We loved it; our home gave the children a chance to come together to run and play.

I kept my focus and rebuked any distractions. Oh, trust me, they formed. I stayed logical. I received my associate degree that month but hadn't walked across the stage yet. What a sigh of relief in victory, I confessed. The urge to walk across the stage delayed my business progress. But it was worth it. Imagine: I once was a high school dropout, but now a college graduate. That fact meant more than money; capital would be there after graduation. I held my head up when I saw my classmates and could tell them I was now a college graduate and a business owner. Success comes in different packages.

The months of 2019 zoomed by. Unfortunately, in the third month, I wasn't the same. We had such a great loss in our family that even today, it isn't the same. Gosh, I wish we didn't have to leave each other in the land of the living. My mind raced; I was filled with questions out the wazoo.

Some of those inquiries were for my grandmothers. Who was easily distracted? Who was hyperactive? Was anyone ADHD? My list went on. It was like the Spirit itself nested in the room and said, "You do not leave yours full of questions. You are free now to do whatever you want to do." Boohooing, I recalled every one of my loved ones as *great*, but now my opportunity arrived; it was up to me to share or bury it.

For me, it started on Snow Hill Road. Reflecting, I realized not everybody's relationship with the Lord starts in the church. At least mine didn't. I was peaceful, full of life, and a loveable little girl. All I ever wanted was an everyday fulfilled life. The day I stood out on the long-paved street. The All-Powerful created a clean heart. The devil knew this. He had to get in the way. When the enemy used a nasty grown man to touch me, I had a heart of forgiveness even then. Although I forgave, it messed me up a bit. It made me dirty. And as life rocked on, what I didn't realize as a young girl was, I was already tough. I only debated with my mom because I didn't know how to communicate. Truthfully, I didn't realize the word *debate* existed. I just knew I had a point to make. My mom's point was, do not go word for word with her. Well, now I know that's what debaters do—they argue. So, what did I do? I just came out and said what I had to say; my mom tried to tell me she didn't want to hear it. She was the mama, end of discussion. However, I wanted her to see my point—that was a trick of the enemy. I could not say then, "Mom, this is a trick of the enemy." I didn't know how. When my mother threatened to take me to the girl's home, I rebelled. I wasn't that bad, and I refused to go to a girls' home, so I ran away. I knew I would be okay. I didn't know how, but I knew I would be fine. Even after all that, my mom and I have the *best* relationship now. She was right; I was the child despite what I thought, felt, or believed. I've learned how to talk to her. Now that I have four daughters, I *definitely* understand motherhood.

I had two daughters who wanted me to work, one who wanted me home, and another who could care less. Therefore, I couldn't spread my wings to fly. I had four baby chicks to protect. With that said, I spread my wings and protected their anointing, by doing what I thought I had to do. When I accomplished what I set out to do, I left Corporate America, the business world, and went home.

Raising four daughters was and is my "mother university" I'm never going to graduate. Excel at maybe, but school is always in session. There have been times when I've had to humble myself and listen to what they had to say—considering that's all I wanted as a kid. Many times, my girls just wanted me to hear their side of the story. When they said I yelled a lot, I had to explain in my defense that I didn't want to put them on punishment, so yelling was the next best thing. And if I said to wash the dishes, wash the dishes. Better yet: don't make me have to tell you, just do it. We worked it out, but as a mother, learning to listen wasn't always easy to do.

No, I wasn't wrong for some of the actions I took. I was wrong the way I did it. For one, my husband was right many times, but I was such an emotional person when it came to my address. Once I got to the root of that, then and only then was I able to confess my faults to myself and my family. If there is no confession, there is no conversion. When decisions had to be made concerning my family, I moved off emotions. When society put pressure on my daughters, they put pressure on me, causing me to pressure my marriage. I never wanted them to do without. And they didn't, but I did. Balling on a budget wasn't but a thing for me. And you know what? I loved it and still love it. I felt better knowing my babies didn't have to go through what I did coming up. "Don't provoke your child to anger" not only means not to make them mad, but also not to spoil them. It was challenging for me to operate in logic. Many times, I had to tell my daughters, "Find joy in guidance." A lot of times, it seemed like I was meaner than a junkyard dog and struck like a rattlesnake, but as their mother, I didn't want them to make some of the same mistakes I made. Looking back, there wasn't anything I couldn't do if I put my mind to it and use my time wisely. I hope I taught them if they feel trapped, use their mind and opportunities to find an escape, always pray, and let the Lord direct their paths.

You know what else I learned in nineteen years? If my spreadsheet would have given me the numbers I wanted, I could have easily seen God or easily heard him speak through my husband or my auntie. But, no, I leaned on my own understanding many times. My excitement got me in trouble. If I only knew then what I know now. I wondered why so many people said that back in the day. Maybe they were like me on occasions: they got in a hurry. I discovered getting in a hurry gets you nowhere. I was blessed to have helped my husband gain assets, but I sure would have enjoyed the moments more without the mulberry bush in my paths. Nevertheless, I got through it. I received a good spanking from the Lord when I didn't accept my calling. I ran for over two years. I needed assurance that it was God choosing me. Now wasn't that foolish...thinking I needed reassurance of doing "good?" The devil sure didn't want me recruiting for the Kingdom of Heaven. Why does it take so long to see that God owns that which is good? The g-o-d in God is the same g-o-d in good.

I didn't have a problem in the workplace, staying logical. That's why I was always able to leave. Throughout my life, looking back, I knew what people wanted in the workplace. My husband and I laughed about me being the undercover employee considering I've had thirteen jobs. And on the business side, I've had eight businesses. He laughed, and I laughed with him, but I was no quitter—I was a go-getter. I did what I had to do as a hustlerett. We need jobs in the world, so I dare not knock the workplace; however, for me, I always knew there was greater. That's why I couldn't stay in one place. I searched high and low, but I never found a job to pay me for my net worth. Don't misunderstand me; I'll get another job if I have to help my family. The point is, in addition, to walking across the stage, the reason I got a business degree is to start in the middle rather than at the bottom. Having a piece of paper on the wall is a good backup.

Appearance is everything. Some can say what they want but do a survey and see. Employers love a confident, classy woman who can excel in customer service. I've been blessed to teach women how to get the job, what to wear to the interview, what to say, and what not to say. Tip #1: It's about how you "talk" to others in addition to doing a great job. It's not about you in the workplace.

Dress for where you want to go, not where you are. Clothes are inexpensive. Take care of your threads. Keep several black pants and change them out with cute tops and cheap accessories, and you'll be amazed where your look can take you. When the supervisor gets upset after customers think you're the head honcho instead of the employee, don't let that upset you. Keep living the life—you're teaching others how to step up their game. Don't we all want the next woman to be *great*? Of course, we do. And a lot of times it starts with appearance, which does not take a whole lot of money.

Speaking on appearance, taking ten minutes out of my day to stretch and exercise helps fulfill that goal. I didn't always have thirty minutes a day, five days a week. But I tell you one thing: it's amazing what ten minutes a day of exercise will do in all areas of your life. When I say exercise, it could be a brisk walk. It's good for your heart and keeps the aches and pains away. Some beats none. Also, if I ate a bunch of junk,

I felt and looked like junk. Many do not believe this, but if you pay attention, you can tell how people take care of themselves inside and out.

One more example that cramps a person's style: the word *um*.

Give me a second, and I'll explain.

When I conversed with people, some could not understand why I hesitated before speaking. (Their facial expressions spoke for them). It wasn't because I was crazy; it was because I wouldn't say I liked using "um" in place of my words. So, I paused and thought about what I had to say. Think about it. If you're in a meeting, class, church, or wherever and every other word the speaker says is "um," it's hard to listen to what the person has to say. Let me help; have someone hold you accountable. If you have that habit, make it fun. Get $10 worth of quarters, and every time you say "um," drop a quarter in a jar. It will help you break the habit, or you'll keep giving $10 away. The beauty of the exercise, *um,* will no longer cramp your style.

From a business standpoint, in 2010 I needed to own a business for tax write-offs and other perks. Having my own business made it about me, unlike the job. Even then I had to care for my customers. There's more flexibility to spend time with family when you own your own business. I chased that more than anything—freedom. There is still work involved, but it's your empire, not someone else's. I didn't mind getting up at 4:00 a.m. to lay brick for my own house.

But when the All-Mighty revealed his version, he tried to tell me in a nutshell, "Not every one of your daughters understands why you are not home, nor does everyone in the workplace understands how you are able to start a job and leave. You cannot run to the workplace, make people fall in love with you, and then leave them. And let's not forget your businesses. You understand what your reasonings are, but your business partners have no idea."

"Wow, God. I so apologize...never in a million years would my pure heart have understood it this way. I get it. You wanted me to acknowledge you in all my ways so you could direct my paths and not just some of my ways. You never had a problem with me doing *good* you had a problem with me not *acknowledging* you."

I didn't realize that God gave me the desire of my heart from 1992 when I said I would never work for anyone all my life. In 1999 when I married my husband, the Almighty fulfilled that desire. Yes, I'd have my own business one day, but I couldn't quite see it God's way, slow and easy. It was easy to see I could be a beauty consultant, an insurance agent, or a saleswoman of other products, but I couldn't see the "good and perfect" setup. You see, I looked for it in a business or a job, but I was my product and service the entire time. I missed it, looking for it.

But now I had arrived at what I had been working toward. On May 9, 2019, I would walk across the stage as a college graduate. I praised God immensely. Sadly, many were not going to attend my ceremony, but it saddened me more because one special person was not going to be there. He supported me in everything. He was there for my first message, my birthday parties, and house parties; he stayed all night; he pooped in my bed; and he had me shouting, "Uncle David, come get him!" He would listen to me talk about his uncle, and he'd never snitch. He looked at me at times, and his facial expression said, "Now, Auntie, you know better than that." I would reply, "Yes, I do, baby." He taught me a valuable lesson: less said is enough sometimes. If anything saddened me that day, it was memories. Auntie loves you, JB. Although you weren't naturally at my graduation, I could see you cheering me on sitting in your red Chevrolet Camaro. You will always have me wrapped around your finger. R.I.P. baby...

Suddenly, my girls yelled down the hallway, "Mom, you want lashes?" and I got my head out of the cloud. I dried my eyes, saying, "Girl, you know I want some lashes." I toughened up like a big girl and walked into the other room to let my daughter put my lashes on. Knowing all was well, I was excited, anxious, proud, grateful, and motivated all day. This hour assured me, if I can do this after all I've been through, I can do anything.

It rained immensely that evening, even flooded in some areas. I understood to the core that many could not be there to cheer me on.

Whoop! Whoop! I couldn't help but to thank God for granting my desire. I know he held the rain back that night for several reasons, but for sure, one reason was for me. Many waded the waters to see me complete one of the greatest accomplishments in my life, and for that, it only gets better for them. I will always be grateful for their love.

The ceremony included 2018–2019 graduates, and here I was sitting in my seat reflecting on the snapshot of my life. I was a woman who wanted and worked to have it all while managing a home life. Not only did I achieve my dream to walk across the stage as a college graduate, but I learned to *balance* it all.

My row stood up and walked behind the curtain. With tears forming but not falling, I was next in line: "Roberta Goffney!" As I walked from behind the curtain, I could hear my babies cheering, my husband shouting, my mom, my Sissy, my forever friend, close family, friends, church family, the ones who watched on the college website, everybody. My smile could not have been any brighter. I wanted to stop and dance, but I couldn't; I had to stay professional. On May 9, 2019, in The Woodlands, Texas, I walked across the stage. This high school dropout is now a college graduate. Whoo-hoo! I did it!

The End

To the Next All-in-One Woman

All-in-One Woman, life is a beautiful art. You have permission to paint your present and your future. If you have to run back into the past, grab the good and keep it moving. Do not stay there. Stay conscious of your present. If you beat yourself up, do it right. Do like I did and *beast* yourself up. Say to yourself, I am tough, and I am not ashamed to own it! When you cry, you tell the universe who you are: "I am a good wife, I am a good mother, I am a good Christian, I am a good friend, I am a good sister, I am all I want to be; I am perfect, 'cause I'm a WOMAN." And when you taste the salt that drips on your lip, let it remind you that life may not always be sweet, but you still need the salt in your batter. You didn't come here to stay; make the best of it. You have the power; it is called patience. Pray, fast, and ask God to help you in whatever your need is. Now, that doesn't mean don't work and believe. Stay consistent. If it's offered to one, it's offered to all. Don't miss it looking for it.

I went all around the mulberry bush so you didn't have to. Please, give time, time. Do not listen to foolish thoughts from the devil. It does not matter if you were a high school dropout, a runaway girl, a drug and alcohol user, a cigarette smoker, or whatever your situation may have been. God will forgive you, and others adore you. There is no other you. There is nothing on this earth that is too hard for God.

Keep this close to your heart. It's one of my favorite scriptures. Every time you need it, use it: "Behold, I am the LORD, the God of all flesh: is there anything too hard for me?" (Jer. 32:27 KJV). Reply, "No, sir." When life gets too busy and you don't know what to do, become productive with God, family, and_____ (your choice). You don't have to experience everything or be in a hurry. That old saying, "What God has for you, it is for you," that's the truth. You just have to go get it. That may simply mean standing up and walking to the next room.

Put him first, try, and be patient. It will come. No matter what you've been praying and believing God for, it's patience that will deliver. Keep in mind, God always uses a mistake(s) for his glory. Am I not living proof? If you have to give the same testimony over and over, so be it. That 10 percent testimony still gives you a reason to praise God and stand tall. Your little bit can go a long way. And never regret being a good mother raising your baby or babies and being a good wife. That is part of God's plan. It doesn't take God long to move. It takes some of us too long to see it.

For all God's children, my blood, and my water, you are God's most treasurable piece on the face of the earth as a human race. Thank you for being my roots. It's a blessing to be you. You are all you need to be. You didn't miss it; you already had him: God, Jesus, and the Holy Ghost.

Now go on and reveal *your* greatness within . . .

To My Grandbabies

Believe it or not, you are the reason for this book. In 2019, I realized a few of you would not know me. I had questions for my grandmothers but never had a chance to ask them. I hope this legacy means as much to you as it did to me.

A few folks are going to say, "Your grandmother, Roberta, was so sweet." Others are going to say, "Yeah, but when she got you behind the closed door alone, she'd chew you out. She'd rip you a new one." Guess what? Both were correct. However, my question is this: how will they tell my story? And for that reason, here you have it—a taste of my hiccups and my straight and narrow.

The *number one* thing I want you to understand is this: the world owes you nothing. The vision I had for myself didn't entirely turn out the way I expected.

However, it was amazing. Loving and committing to my responsibilities remained my priority. When I thought about it, I didn't have to love and commit to my responsibilities, but I wouldn't have been able to live with myself. That said, think about it: God does not have to be a good God. He does not have to have mercy on humans, nor does he have to do anything.

I rest my case.

It is best if you remember, once you have a family or baby, your life is no longer your own. It's no longer "about you." But it's exciting to know that you're on the receiving end.

With that said, you can still have peace and joy being a spouse or raising your babies. The magic pill is *patience*. Just because you don't get it this month doesn't mean you can't have it next year. But hear me well, if you rush the process, that year can turn into a decade.

As life journeys on, you'll notice some people in the world have a habit of saying certain cliches. As your granny, I didn't, nor do I say what everyone else says or do what everyone else does. For example, some have a habit of saying, "Everyone is going through something." I wish they wouldn't speak for me. I was not "always" going through something. You see the difference? I had blessed, exciting, and joyful days. To me, a person is what he or she believes they are. Why do we smile if we are always going through? Why do we encourage others if we are always going through something? Do you get my drift? The world is not always clear. This is where your understanding *must* kick in.

If my girlfriend knew I was with her last night and someone said I robbed the bank, then she should speak for me in defense of my innocence. Know when and when not to speak for others. After a while, the thing called life becomes common sense to the individual. Don't get tangled up in cliches. The world means well, but some forget that there is power in the tongue.

One of my most powerful possessions was knowing who I was, not what I had.

And one last thing, if you can read, you can cook. Taking care of your family doesn't have to be detrimental. Simply read recipes and tweak them if you must. If you're new in the kitchen, stick to the recipe, and learn from the experience. Make it a habit to read everywhere you go. When you walk into the doctor's office, and there's a post on the wall, please read it. The same applies to the grocery stores; read the flyer (s) on the door. From now on, read as many words as you see. Your brain is a muscle that needs exercise, and reading is the best exercise for your brain. You may not have the privilege to read long periods in a day but start with five to ten minutes. I understand being pregnant, having one baby on your hip, another in the highchair, and one screaming your name from the other room; time may not be on your side. However, I promise you can find five to ten minutes to exercise that muscle (brain). You can do it! I'm cheering for you all the way! If you really want to enjoy the text, read that which interests you. Go to the library (whenever you have a chance) relax for ten minutes reading over that topic. Five words turn into fifty, fifty turn into a hundred, and so on. Trust me, reading matters. Besides, you're reading your Bible, aren't you?

That said, have a blessed day. And remember, Glams said, "Life is about the decisions you make."

Granny's Quotes That Kept Granny Strong

- Life is about the decisions you make.
- When I lived in the sunshine, someone else was in the rain. And when I was in the rain, someone else was in the sunshine.
- Do not expect people to understand what they haven't lived.
- It's easy for someone to bring you down to their standards, but it's challenging to bring them up to yours.
- If the shoe fits, change them. New creatures don't wear old shoes.
- If the writing is on the wall, don't paint over it. Respect it and keep it moving.
- Love in spite of.
- Let your life speak for you.
- If you eat a bunch of junk, you'll feel like junk.
- If you're eager to say it, write it down. If you forget, it probably wasn't meant to be repeated.
- "It's not what you say; it's how you say it."
- "It's not what you do; it's how you do it."
- Always cheer for others' success. Your day will come.

- God's creatures, human beings—can't live with them, and can't live without them.
- You can't always teach talking, and you can't always teach silent.
- Stay balanced and focus.
- I can't deny what I know but will not bulk up to what I don't.
- If you must compete, only compete with yourself—unless you are in a sport that "competes." Have fun! And remember, you lose some and you win some.
- You have what it takes to start something great.
- It's better to live knowing Christ than to die having denied him.

REVEALING THE GREATNESS WITHIN: PART 2

Uncle Terry Earl, I was a little bitty thing when you passed. One night I remember clear as day I saw you walking toward me. I cried and told God, "I do not want to see dead people." I was seven years of age. My mother said I had a bad dream. That night and many after that, I did not want to have any more bad dreams. You were such a *great* uncle; it took me a long time to get over your death. I'll always love you, uncle T.
R.I.P.
May 5, 1961 - May 30, 1980

Revealing the Greatness Within: Part 2

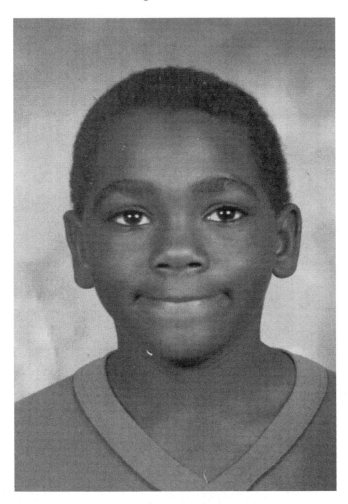

Thank you, little brother, for being the best student a big sister could ever have. I didn't have you long on earth, but I valued every second I did. Only God knows what's best for us. You were a *great* kid who appreciated the little things in life, and I love you indefinitely, Willie Jr., a. k. a. Duke.
R.I.P.
February 1, 1978 – May 1988

Thank you, papa, and granny, for being outstanding role models. You two were a great team together; I hope I can walk in your shoes, grandmother. Love you, eternally.
R.I.P.
Papa Henry Sr.
February 6, 1920 - December 18, 1992
Granny Dorothy
April 19, 1928 - March 17, 1996

Revealing the Greatness Within: Part 2

Grandpa Henry, a. k. a. Plutie, you were such a great poet. It's because of you I like to rhyme from time to time. Thank you, papa, for all the days you made me feel special as your granddaughter. I will forever love you.
R.I.P.
February 6, 1920 - December 18, 1992

Papa Henry's Sr. and Grandma Dorothy's daughter Ella:

Oh, Sookie, Sookie. Thank you, Aunt Ella, for teaching me how to use lipstick as eyeshadow. You were not the auntie I mentioned in the story; I wanted to save this page for you. One thing I loved about our relationship the most is how we danced! It's because of you I love different hairstyles. You rocked your natural hair, and when you wanted a change, you'd put on a wig. Thank you for letting us be little girls and play with your expensive hairpiece. You were a *great* woman, and I'll always cherish our relationship.

R.I.P.

Aunt Ella.

October 17, 1953 - March 29, 1994

My beautiful chocolate chip, Mrs. Dorothy Williams, your skin was always rejuvenating. Thank you immensely, granny, for your words of wisdom. You were such a *great* woman. You will forever be in my heart.
R.I.P.
April 19, 1928 - March 17, 1996

David Jr.'s Grandmother Mittie Pearl Edmond,
thank you for encouraging us girls always to keep a
snack in our purse. I love you, Granny.
R.I.P.
January 1, 1921 - June 2007

Revealing the Greatness Within: Part 2

Oh, Grandma Evelyn, you loved a little bling; even this blouse has shimmer in it. I get it from the Thompson side. A little *shine* makes a girl feel better. I see you eating one of our favorite fruits, a plum; you were right, granny. If my husband treats me right, hang in there. I love you immensely.
R.I.P.
October 3, 1936 - August 30, 2005

David Jr.'s Grandpa Ralph Lewis Sr. We had a good time at Aunt Lizzy's and Uncle Miller's house drinking coffee. Oh, what a time...
I love you, papa.
R.I.P.
July 26, 1929 – August 22, 2008

Revealing the Greatness Within: Part 2

Aunt Iva, we had many laughs talking about our similarities. Your smile was so radiant; you always said I had your feet, and you were right; I do. What else did we say, "He's not marrying me for my feet!" Thank you, auntie, for keeping it real. I'll always treasure our relationship.
R.I.P.
May 1958 – 2009

Grandma Minter, David Jr.'s grandmother. Oh, Grandma, how I miss our holidays. I loved it when you said, "Lett, cut me a *lit-e-piece* of that onion to go with these greens and cornbread." You were such a noblewoman of God; I miss you, granny, and I love you to infinity.
R.I.P.
April 9, 1930 - September 13, 2014

Revealing the Greatness Within: Part 2

My Sweet Daddy, you were a good man from where you stood. I did not hold you accountable for how my life turned out. You know why? Whatever I wanted, I had the power to earn it. You did your part when you gave me life, and for that, I'm grateful. By the way, David Jr. is doing an extraordinary job taking care of me. I know you were not too happy in 1999, but all is well; we're still going strong. I love you so much, daddy; you are forever in my heart.
R.I.P.
April 15, 1951 - May 29, 2015

Me and my daddy
R.I.P. Mr. Willie Thompson Sr

Oh, Auntie's Baby, JB, how you had me wrapped around your little finger.
Roses are red. Violets are blue; no one had my heart like you.
You could have run in my house and jumped all day, and none of us would have had a word to say.
Words can't express how I feel; I love you forever, and that's for real.
R.I.P.
Mr. Joseph O. Goffney, Jr.
December 21, 1999 - March 6, 2019

Me in the middle, Baby S'Kiya, David Jr. (Left) Jarvis Jr., Shanyira, Sanshae, Santavia (My oldest daughter the bride), Jarvis Sr. (Husband), Shantel and Shani'ya

Welcome to the world, baby Selah. We love you!!!

My mother, in her younger days, you were a cutie-patootie mother!!! Go ahead and work it. She's the reason I love to put my hands on my hips.

Forever my Sunshine Lady, my lovely mother, Alice.

Thank you, Papa Dennis, for taking great care of my mother for nearly thirty years. You have immensely been a man of your word. Keep living the life, papa. I appreciate your words of wisdom; I thank God I haven't had to work on a car yet, but you gave me some great survival tips if I ever have to.

Revealing the Greatness Within: Part 2

This is my stunning mother-in-law, Cedell and my handsome father-in-law David L. Sr.

That's our queen in the middle, our mother. We love you, nonstop, mom. All four of us will forever be a team to make your dreams a reality.
(left) My baby sister Monalisa, me, my mom, my oldest sister Priscilla, and my second oldest sister Alicia.

Revealing the Greatness Within: Part 2

It's a blessing to have siblings.
(Left) Alicia, my oldest brother, Thee, Priscilla, mom, Monalisa, and me.

Made in the USA
Columbia, SC
14 February 2021

32422523R00145